BUDGETARY SUPERVISION IN CHINA

An Institutional Perspective of Provincial People's Congress

BUDGETARY SUPERVISION IN CHINA

An Institutional Perspective of Provincial People's Congress

Shujian Zhang
Fudan University, China

World Century

Published by

World Century Publishing Corporation
27 Warren Street, Suite 401-402, Hackensack, NJ 07601

Library of Congress Cataloging-in-Publication Data
Zhang, Shujian, 1978–
Budgetary supervision in China : an institutional perspective of provincial people's congress / by Zhang Shujian (Fudan University, China).
pages cm
Includes bibliographical references and index.
ISBN 978-1-938134-56-2 (alk. paper)
1. Finance, Public--State supervision--China. 2. Intergovernmental fiscal relations--China. 3. People's councils--China. I. Title.
HJ1408.Z435 2015
328.51'07456--dc23
2014033597

British Library Cataloguing-in-Publication Data
A catalogue record for this book is available from the British Library.

In-house Editors: Dong Lixi/Parvath Radha

Typeset by Stallion Press
Email: enquiries@stallionpress.com

Printed in Singapore by Mainland Press Pte Ltd.

Contents

About the Author

Dr. Shujian Zhang is an Assistant Professor at school of social development and public policy, Fudan University, China. He received his Ph.D. degree in 2011 at Law School of Fudan University and is also a research fellow at China Center for Economic Studies (CCES), Fudan University and a research fellow at Shanghai–HongKong Development Institute, Fudan University. He focuses his academic interests on Chinese provincial politics, local governance, fiscal constitutionalism and public policy fields. He was ever a research assistant in East Asian Institute of National University of Singapore and a postdoctoral fellow at McCourt School of Public Policy of Georgetown University.

Introduction

The National and local People's Congress at various levels are the national and local organs of power in China. According to the Chinese system of Constitution and laws, except the highest powers of law-making, decision-making, and appointment, the People's Congress also has the highest power of supervision over the government. The supervision over the government behaviors by the People's Congress can be summarized in two categories: one is to supervise the plans and budgets and the other is to supervise the government responsibilities. Financial supervision includes three aspects — examination and approval of the national and local economic plans and budgets; supervision over implementation of the plans and budgets; and examination and approval of adjustment and changes of some plans and budgets in the course of implementation.[1] Therefore, budgetary supervision is an important statutory function of the People's Congress at all levels.

Throughout the 1980s, China's fiscal system underwent many important changes, transferring from a concentrated budget revenue allocation system fully controlled by the central government into relatively decentralized institutional arrangements. Compared with the central government, the provincial governments had advantage in information in meeting local needs so that they can provide better public goods and services, which in turn have great impacts on local economic environments.[2] The proportion of local fiscal expenditure has been steadily rising in the course of the fiscal contract system and tax-sharing reform. Local governments

[1] Cai Ding-jian. *The People's Congress System in China* (Fourth Edition), Beijing: Law Press, 2003: 376–378.

[2] Lin Yi-fu, Liu Zhi-qiang. China's Financial Decentralization and Economic Growth. *Journal of Peking University* (*Philosophy and Social Science*), 2000, (6): 13.

obtain ever-increasing powers of financial control and their financial behavior variables have great impact on efficiency of expenditure and service orientation of the public finances. It seems that China has already been an extremely financially decentralized nation.

However, on the one hand, the quality of public services is subject to allocations of tax between the governments and on the other, it is directly supervised and restricted by the voters. Fiscal decentralization of the grass-roots government provides solutions to the public's preferences for information and public supervision, that is to say, closer the government is to the service objects, easier it is for it to be supervised by the voters. In China, public supervision has not been the main force of standardizing local governments to provide public services and thus fiscal decentralization is limited to a certain degree.[3] This is determined by the particular political and economic environments in China. Chinese economic and social development greatly relies on non-budgetary funds and government revenues and expenditures have blind spots, which is harmful to fair public services provided by local governments. Economists universally believe that non-budgetary and budgetary financial resources have different, or even reverse, influences on the efficiency of government expenditures. In order to meet the country's financial transformation and improve legal construction, China must explore a road to budgetary democracy with advancing of the budgetary supervision system of the People's Congress at its core.

Considering the legislative authority system in China, budgetary democracy with budgetary supervision of the People's Congress at the core can be constructed starting from the provincial system. In the Chinese legislative system consisting of the Constitution, laws, administrative regulations, local regulations, autonomous regulations, and specific regulations and rules, provinces (including large cities) are grassroots government units with legislative power and the provincial governments are at the intermediate level in Chinese political hierarchy. Provincial governments have a direct power of unified leadership in various regions that greatly differ in their economic and social development, while only the

[3] Zhou Li-an. *Local Government in Transformation — Incentives and Governance of the Officials*, Shanghai: Shanghai People's Publishing House, 2008: 55.

municipal People's Congress and governments of big cities can play a leading role in the development of the regions. So construction of the provincial budgetary supervision system will have a greater impact on the Chinese society.

In the entire national fiscal system, the provincial government budget is an extremely important part as it has both self-determined powers of regional legislation and great capacity for financial co-ordination. After the tax-sharing reform in 1994, the local People's Congress became more conscious of supervising the government budgets and every province had legislative power in budgetary supervision. The People's Congress of all provinces have made local laws and regulations such as decrees and rules in the examination and supervision of the budget because systems that are relatively perfect and practical in implementation have positive impact on the province's economic and social development, thus evolving competition between the provinces to a certain extent. Compilation and implementation of provincial government budgets are so complicated compared with that of the central government budget, and thus studies of budgetary supervision of provincial People's Congress are of greater importance for promoting the function of the local People's Congress and efficiency of the local governments.

Section 1. Putting Forward the Topic under Discussion and its Value in Research

1. Background for Putting Forward the Topic under Discussion

Data provided in the World Development Report of governments in the changing world in 1997 shows that in developed countries, the provincial (state) governments' financial expenditures are about 30% on average of the total expenditures of governments at the various levels and the percentage is just 60% even in the most decentralized countries such as Canada and Japan. In the 1990s, the average percentage in developing countries was 14%, in the transitional economies 26%, and in the United States less than 50%. In China, provincial fiscal expenditures keep nearly 70% of the total national fiscal expenditures since over a decade.[4] On the

[4] Zhang Jun. *The Reform Unknown to the Public*, Beijing: CITIC Publishing House, 2010: 140–141.

one hand, the percentage of Chinese local government financial expenditure is extremely high but on the other hand public supervision is not complete or perfect.

After the tax-sharing reform in 1994, the central and local governments did not make satisfactory division and coordination in administrative and financial powers and the scale of revenues and expenditures was continuously expanding as the local governments were taking more and more responsibilities while they were not allowed to raise loans as definitely prescribed by the current laws and regulations in China. The local government generally raised loans from banks or other institutions by establishing a financing platform, namely investment and financing companies and in the name of the companies, thus forming a large number of hidden debts.

Liu Ming-kang, the chairman of China Banking Regulatory Commission (CBRC) reported on the second CBRC economic and financial situation analysis bulletin meeting in 2010 that by the end of 2009, the loan balance of the local government financing platform was 7.38 trillion Yuan, with an increase of 70.4%. It was 20.4% of the general loans and the new loan was 3.05 trillion Yuan in the year, 34.5% of new general loans. It is very close to the international warning line of 60% widely recognized throughout the world.[5] The amount of local government debt estimated by experts and scholars is larger than the amount released officially. If such a large scale of financial revenues and expenditures are not subject to strong supervision for a long time the trend is very dangerous.

As local debts are not included in the budget, the use of debt funds is not effectively constrained and the debts are neither transparent nor normative, and the local governments are burdened with more and more debts with the economic and social development. In fact the situation and scale of the debts is obviously against the laws in China. Article 28 of the Budget Law expressly states that the local budgets at various levels shall be compiled according to the principles of keeping expenditures within the limits of revenues and maintaining a balance between revenues and expenditures, and shall not contain deficit. The local governments may not

[5] Local Debts at Risk — to Get rid of Institutional Obstacles in Local Government Economic Development is the Basic Solution. *China Business Times*, 2010.

issue local government bonds, unless prescribed by laws or the State Council.

Li Jin-hua, former Auditor-General of the National Office of Audit once in the audit report pointed out that in some cases fake expenditures at the central level were added to the subsidies of local expenditures arranged in the budget of expenditures at the central level at the beginning of a year and the use of these funds is not managed or supervised by the local governments and the People's Congress. In some provinces compilation of the budgets and final accounts of central subsidies to local revenues is incomplete. The part of the central subsidies not included in the budgets actually is not examined and supervised by the local People's Congress.[6] Non-budgetary finance occupies a more and more important position in the local financial revenues and expenditures.

The reason why local officials dare to increase debts is absence of a supervision mechanism. Excessive debts should have been constrained by budgets while the funds that the government obtains by raising loans are not included in the budgets, and on the contrary are used beyond the budgets. Besides, currently the local People's Congress has very low capacity in supervising government budgets. Naturally some local officials do not seriously consider the negative impacts of expansive debts as they are eager to show high performance in the limited term to obtain opportunities for promotion. Non-budgetary funds have become mobile financial powers and rights of local governments and departments given by the state to stimulate their initiative to achieve economic development and engage in profit-making activities.[7]

The tax-sharing mode below the provincial level just existed nominally after the tax-sharing system reform in 1994 and local governments below the provincial level highly rely on non-budgetary funds and funds beyond the system as they have no freedom in income and there is no formal income transfer mechanism. Non-budgetary revenues and expenditures are mainly kept by the local governments (90% or more) and nearly 40% of the

---

[6] Li Jin-hua. Auditing Report on Implementation of the Central Budget and Other Financial Revenues and Expenditures in 2003. Communique of the Tenth Meeting of the Tenth Standing Committee of the National People's Congress, 2004.

[7] Zhou Li-an. *Local Government in Transformation — Incentives and Governance of the Officials*, Shanghai: Shanghai People's Publishing House, 2008: 182.

revenues of the local governments come from non-tax income. A great number of financial resources are not included in the budgets, thus forming non-budgetary funds and funds beyond the system. Although they have positive impacts on the infrastructure construction of local governments and on the promotion of local economic development, they undermine the government's budget constraints and budget integrity, leading to random and non-normative acts of the governments, thus making public funds free of strong supervision and providing opportunities for corruption.[8]

Furthermore, non-budgetary funds are various charges and fees coming from enterprises, farmers, and urban residents and their scale greatly differ in different regions.[9] They enlarge the gaps of per capita expenditure and per capita public services levels in the regions. This implies the great damages caused by non-budgetary funds to China's financial system and its negative impacts on construction of a legal society as the governments at the provincial levels truly undertake the responsibilities of maintaining social development and providing fair services. The whole society of China would pay extremely high costs in the system if it is not controlled in finance and legislation. Besides, the danger of such a financial crisis has become obvious in the formal investigation reports of inner audit departments of Chinese governments in recent years.

Liu Jia-yi, auditor general of the Audit Administration, when making reports on implementation of central budgets of 2009 and audit of other financial revenues and expenditures to the standing committee of the National People's Congress on June 23, 2010, pointed out that the debts of the local governments were incurred a long time ago and were on a large scale. Compilation and reporting of local budgets and final accounts, and management of tax and fees are not strict enough with some local financial resources loosely managed. From January 2008 to June 2009, according to the audits and investigations made in 17 provinces, 79.416 billion Yuan of non-tax revenues that should be collected were not collected and in some regions the governments even returned 13.036 billion Yuan of tax and fees

---

[8] Liu Shou-gang. *Financial Logic of National Growth — Financial Transformation and Political Development in Modern China*, Tianjin: Tianjin People's Publishing House, 2009: 306.

[9] Zhou Li-an. Local Government in Transformation — Incentives and Governance of the Officials, Shanghai: Shanghai People's Publishing House, 2008: 178–179.

to enterprises or individuals in the name of the policies made by them. In these regions, except the state treasury deposit accounts, the financial departments at the provincial level made 1197 accounts in commercial banks, of which 920 should be removed or merged, which amounts to more than 50 in each province in average, and this sort of distributed storage is not in favor of overall management and use of funds.[10]

The scope and depth of public expenditures is mostly determined by government officials rather than public voting. As to the budget system, the most important in the financial system, the most serious problem of China's budget system is the lack of a complete and unified public budget covering the revenues and expenditures of all governments. It originates from a large number of non-budgetary funds that are not constrained by the budget law.[11] The negative effects caused by the imperfect management system of non-budgetary funds has drawn attention of the central government, which will encourage local governments at all levels to standardize the budget management system and urge the local People's Congress at all levels to strengthen the budgetary supervision.

In 1996, the State Council promulgated the Decision on Strengthening the Management of Non-budgetary Funds, in which the most outstanding part is to have non-budgetary funds included in the financial budget management. All the additional taxes and fees charged by the local financial departments according to the national regulations would be included in local budgets as local financial fixed income rather than non-budgetary funds from 1996 onwards. The decision also proposed to gradually manage the non-budgetary budgets that should be included in the management of the financial budget. This shows that it has been the direction of reform to abolish non-budgetary funds.[12]

Provincial People's Congress is the primary legislative organ of state power to supervise financial budgets of the provincial finance and the

---

[10] Audit Bureau: Some Local Governments under Great Pressure of Debts. Auditing Results of Financial Management in 17 Provinces and Municipalities (Audit Report No. 12 of 2010), 2010.

[11] Deng Yu-Wen. Audit Storm Urging Budget Reform. *International Finance*, 2005, 7 (4): 5.

[12] Yang Zhi-yong, Yang Zhi-gang. *30 Years of Reform of Financial System in China*, Shanghai: Shanghai People's Publishing House, 2008: 118–119.

governments at various levels below province and it is very important to institutionalize and standardize its power of budgetary supervision. The provincial People's Congress does make great progress in the budgetary supervision system after years of development, especially after the reform of local budgets. In the 1980s, many local People's Congress and the standing committee made normative regulations on budgetary supervision or defined specific contents of budgetary supervision in relevant normative documents according to the specific conditions in their provinces. For example, in 1988, Anhui enacted Interim Measures for Budget Management which details principal rules for partial change of the budgets and makes it operational in practice. The People's Congress of Sichuan, Hebei, Chongqing, Hefei, and many other provinces, cities, and counties (districts) also make regulations on budgets. These initiatives mark standardization and institutionalization of exercise of powers of budgetary supervision at the local level.[13]

After the tax-sharing reform in 1994, the People's Congress of various provinces are more conscious of supervision over government budgets and all of them have made local regulations such as decrees or rules for examination and supervision of budgets. However, these systems exposed during operation a common flaw that supervision is rather procedural than substantive. For various reasons provincial People's Congress failed to truly meet the requirements of supervision over public revenues and expenditures based on the principles of financial democracy and the requirements of decision-making powers. The limited content of the power of budgetary supervision is not complete. The contents, scope, and operating norms of the system need further improvement and the laws on budgetary supervision are too general.

2. Theoretical Basis of the Topic and its Significance

Constitutional system protects citizens' fundamental rights, and governments are the authorities directly bearing the responsibility. If the

[13] Ren Xi-rong. Budget Supervision and Financial Democracy: Growth of the Power of Budget Supervision of the People's Congress. *Journal of University of Political Science of East China*, 2009, (5): 104.

Constitution cannot organize an effective, publicly supported government which can complete tax-collecting and expenditures affairs, it will fail to protect rights in practice. Any government opponent will never be a member of the group that supports the rights of individuals as the rights can be well-exercised only with pressure from governments and with public funds.[14] However, carry on its functions, the government needs financial support, or it will not achieve the basic purpose of protecting the basic rights of citizens such as the right of property. Therefore, the joint public funds of citizens must be utilized to pay for the night watchman, that is, the government. In other words, if there are no taxes, then there is no property. Both the right of welfare and the right of private property have public costs. The public costs of freedom of contract are not less than those of health care and the public costs of freedom of expression are not less than those of the right of decent housing. All rights need support of public funds.[15]

Considering the history of development of constitutionalism, constraints against arbitrary power based on finance is the foundation for the establishment and development of constitutionalism. Representatives originated from the cities in Western Europe in the Middle Ages, mainly for the needs of construction of urban public finance. Because of the feudal system in the Middle Ages, autonomy of the Western European cities required all citizens to work together to defend their cities. This led to the formation of representative democracy to organize and manage common defense funds, which was a major innovation in financial institution.[16]

Representative democracy provides the basis of institutional framework and organization for construction of public finance. The modern budget system first appeared in England, coinciding with the appearance of the parliamentary and the center of parliamentary authority generated in the process of supervising financial powers of the king by representative agencies. Parliament is a prerequisite of the organizational system of

---

[14] Stephen Holmes, Keith Sunstein. *Costs of Rights — Why Freedom Depends on Tax*, Beijing: Peking University Press, 2004: 37.

[15] Stephen Holmes, Keith Sunstein. *Costs of Rights — Why Freedom Depends on Tax*, Beijing: Peking University Press, 2004: 3.

[16] Wei Jian-guo. *Formation of Constitutional System and Rise of Modern Britain*, Beijing: Law Press, 2006: 106.

the national budget and an organization restricting the authoritarian.[17] The principle of no taxation without representative was eventually established in the process of supervision over the king's tax collection by the representative agencies, reflecting victory of the representative agencies in supervising the king's right of tax collection and marking the beginning of parliamentarianism.

Public finance emphasized the publicity of the state functions and financial functions in essence which originates from common needs of the human beings. The public society cannot individually afford the high expenditures of public facilities and costs of management. Government cannot normally run without a large number of funds and everyone who is protected should pay the portion of expenditure from his business to maintain his government. But it still needs his consent, that is, consent of the majority or the representatives they elected.[18] The Bill of Rights in 1689 clearly stated: The right of financial management permanently belongs to the Parliament; anyone cannot be forced to pay taxes or other charges unless agreed by the Parliament by passing a bill and the total expenditure of the king should be approved by the Parliament.[19]

Financial budget can ensure normal operation of state power at all levels, guarantee its legitimacy and authority, dominate the government's behaviors by controlling expenditures of the governments at various levels and attract maximum of the citizens as participant of budgets in supervising government behavior, which is one of the most important constitutionalism to ensure and constrain state power in the constitutional mode. Therefore, the starting point of promoting China's current constitutionalism is the construction of a democratic budgetary system. In the democratic system of budget, government behaviors of the revenues and expenditures are supervised by the people and their representative agencies. In this budgetary system, the government budgets are politically controlled from the outside so that government budgets can perform public responsibility.

---

[17] Wang Shi-tao. Constitutional Interpretation of Chinese Finance. *Journal of Gansu Political Science and Law Institute*, 2008, (2): 32.

[18] Locke. *Theory of Government* (*Part II*), Beijing: Commercial Press, 1964: 88.

[19] Liu Jian-wen. The Finance under Rule of Law from the Democratic Perspective, Beijing: Peking University Press, 2006: 184.

If the People's Congress can substantively supervise government budgets, it can be a power of check and balance of government and can constrain the governments' predatory behaviors in revenues to a certain degree and cut down waste and corruption of government expenditures, thus prompting the governments to spend revenues on things in favor of the people. Budgetary democracy can also help improve management of government budget and make the state systems more rational.[20] In China, about 70% of public expenditures are spent by the governments at provincial or lower levels, and the provincial government is a political hub with legislative powers so that explorations of approaches to budgetary democracy based on budgetary supervision of the People's Congress can start from the provincial government as a pilot for provision of legislative foundations.

3. Issues to Be Addressed

After the introduction of the fiscal contract system in 1988, the central government basically ended the responsibilities of providing funds for local expenditures. The functions of local governments were transferred from providing services to raising funds for the services which means the process of decentralization of administrative power. After formal establishment of the tax-sharing system in 1994, the responsibilities of expenditures of the local governments were stipulated in the Budget Law. Financial budgets of the provincial governments were extremely important as they have both autonomy and capacity of overall planning. Unfortunately, they have no autonomy or freedom in tax collection and they actively expand non-budgetary income for maximum benefit after decentralization of administrative powers and under such a context, supervision of financial revenues and expenditures is getting more and more important. The tax-sharing system reform in 1994 did not propose an income distribution pattern for the governments below provincial level and it determines that supervision over provincial budget is an important part of China's legal construction concerning national capacities, which highlights the theoretical and practical significance of this book.

---

[20] Ma Jun. *Chinese Public Budget Reform: Rationalization and Democratization*, Central Compilation and Translation Press, 2005: 55.

Viewed from the current situation, examinations of the People's Congress on the budgets in the process of compiling budgets are actually rather formalistic or routine than substantive, and supervision in the process of implementing budgets is rather ratified than punitive. The main purpose of this book is to clarify a series of issues involving the democratic system of the local budget from the perspective of substantive supervision of the local People's Congress with emphasis on analysis of issues, involving democratic outline and system, to be solved for reaching the goal of substantial supervision by checking, analyzing, and comparing the current supervision system of the provincial budget in China. Promotion of construction of budgetary democracy has positive impacts on legitimacy and authority of the governments at all levels and enables the governments to reform their administrative management, thus constructing governments that are responsible and ruled by law.

A provincial Party committee has great decision-making power in public financial revenues and expenditures and its supervision by the People's Congress is an important field to be explored, requiring checks and balances and cooperation on budgets among the Party committee, the People's Congress, and the government based on the current political structure. Promotion of budgetary democracy will guide the direction of reform of the entire political system and has significant impacts on the political position of the People's Congress and the political power structure. Serious consideration should be given to the relationship between the People's Congress and the ruling Party; in fact, the political position of the People's Congress should be redefined in the current political structure.

As to the use of public funds, it seems that representatives and parliamentary members can be predatory by opportunism as government officials do. Besides, in order to be in favor of interest groups or for other considerations, the deputies to the People's Congress may have the same incentives to spend money for plundering public funds than government officials do.[21] In the countries in which the system of budgetary supervision by the People's Congress is relatively perfect throughout the world, the power of budgetary supervision is strictly constrained. Systems should

[21] Zeng Jun-ping. The Budget Amendment Rights Need Strict Rules and Norms. *Journal of Shanghai University of Finance and Economics*, 2008, (3): 54.

be designed to prevent expansion of the budgetary powers of the People's Congress and too much interference in the executive power, which negatively influence the efficiency of government operation. In this book, explorations are made on the exercise of supervisory powers of the Provincial People's Congress.

Budget information is the basis of budgetary supervision and the budgetary supervision system can normally function if there is full disclosure of budget information. But currently the provincial budget information disclosure system and the budgetary supervision system are not well-coordinated; even the laws and regulations on budget are not sound in terms of integrity and effectiveness. Therefore, it should discuss not only improving the right to know on budgetary information from the perspective of Constitution but also institutionalizing and standardizing the system of budgetary information disclosure.

Budgetary supervision is some sort of procedural supervision and it is difficult for the People's Congress to substantially supervise the government budgetary behaviors if there is no substantive provision defining the process of supervision in the provincial budgetary supervision system. In the current system, the provincial People's Congress does not have the right to amend the draft budget and cannot actively take part in supervising the process of implementing budgets. Therefore, explorations should be made in strengthening supervision over the whole process of budgets by the People's Congress, improving legislation and intensifying citizens' participation and supervision, thus really providing the People's Congress with legal functions of supervising the budgetary process and protecting the fundamental rights of citizens.

Section 2. Summary and Evaluation of the Researches

The field of the budgetary supervision system of the provincial People's Congress should be not only studied from theories of law, politics, and economics but also analyzed with a large number of empirical materials. Given the great differences in economic and social development between the provinces in China, comparison of the differences in making and implementing regulations in different regions is also a necessary content to be studied. Finally, researches into the system should be compared and analyzed based on studies in all disciplines to explore how to develop a supervising system suitable for local development and its mode of operation. Studies on systems at the provincial level in China are rarely done by political and legal researchers abroad and most are done only by domestic scholars.

1. Analysis from the Perspective of Constitutional Principle and the Power of Budgetary Supervision

The first thing to be clarified regarding the budgetary supervision of the People's Congress is the meaning of power separation from the legal perspective. China's Constitution provides that the National People's Congress and the local People's Congress at various levels are the organs through which the people exercise state power. The people administer state affairs and manage economic, cultural, and social affairs through various channels and in various ways in accordance with the laws. The local People's Congress at and above the county levels shall examine and approve the plans for economic and social development and the budgets of their respective administrative areas, and examine and approve the reports on their implementation. The researches made by the professors Liu Jian-wen and Xiong Wei from Beijing University are mainly focused on legal analysis of constitutional significance of budgetary supervision of the People's Congress.

The core power of the People's Congress is the power of supervision. In accordance with the laws, regulations and rules, it supervises every step of the process of government revenues and expenditures, representing the concept of public finance by law. Financial supervision increasingly comes into the field of view and becomes the focus of attention while the process of legalization is deepening further in China. The nature of financial supervision is to constrain and regulate government powers, making the government act financially in accordance with the laws and regulations. Therefore, the extent of financial supervision reflects the status of the game between the Parliament and the government. In the whole financial supervision system, the power of budgetary supervision of the Parliament is undoubtedly the most important and of essential authority.[22]

[22] Liu Jian-wen. *The Finance under Rule of Law from the Democratic Perspective*, Beijing: Peking University Press, 2006: 184.

2. Analysis from the Perspective of Democratization and Rationalization of Provincial Public Budget and Budgetary Reform

Researches on the provincial budgetary supervision system is a field of study involving laws, politics, and economics in which a large number of empirical studies should be made based on full theoretical argumentation for finding the bases of the system construction. Such a methodology of research is rarely used by traditional Chinese scholars in general. The research teams led by Professor Ma Jun from Sun Yat-sen University and Professor Jiang Hong from Shanghai University of Finance and Economics are the main teams which initiated research in this area and have rich academic achievements. The nature of public budget is political and the core issue existing in budget is the game between public powers and civil rights with the most critical relationship linked by the People's Congress. The balance between the various powers actually constitutes a system that needs assessing and reasoning so as to finally achieve the goal of rule of law. The two research teams noted the importance of comparative and empirical researches in this field and collected a large number of data at the provincial level that were gathered and analyzed for researches from different angles with the same research direction of democratization of provincial budget reform.

It is very common to study budgetary democracy from the perspective of state power. Budgetary democracy would weaken the state administrative control of the budget but it can also bring financial and political benefits to the state, because the taxpayers will cooperate in determining financial budget, thus contributing to a steady growth of revenues and increase of legitimacy of the regime.[23] Upon achieving budgetary democracy, the government's budget will be disclosed to the whole society and supervised by the People's Congress, which will throw pressure on the government to improve budgetary management. Certainly, the People's Congress should be well organized for strong supervision over government budgets. The relationship between the People's Congress and the ruling Party must be more reasonably constructed to solve the problems of the deputies to the People's Congress.

---

[23] Ma Jun. *Chinese Public Budget Reform: Rationalization and Democratization*. Central Compilation and Translation Press, 2005: 48.

3. Analysis from the Perspective of Disclosure of Financial Information

On the 17th National Congress of the CCP, it was proposed to improve the democratic system; enrich the forms of democracy; expand democratic channels; carry out democratic election, democratic decision-making, democratic management, and democratic supervision; and guarantee the people's rights to know, to participate, to express and to supervise. In these four specific rights, the right to know is put at the first position. Government information disclosure is not only an act to restrain government behavior but also a necessary measure to encourage government as transparency of financial information is the basis of disclosure of other government information. Domestic studies of budget information disclosure were mainly carried out by the team of Professor Jiang Hong, Zeng Jun-ping, Xu Shu-na and so on from Shanghai University of Finance and Economics, who issued a "Report on China's Fiscal Transparency — The Evaluation of Provincial Fiscal Information Disclosure" in 2009. Data of provincial final accounts were chosen for survey in which openness and availability of fiscal information were regarded as the basic criteria to be evaluated and emphases were laid on the following aspects: provincial financial information's degree of openness, scope, and specific degree. Financial transparency of various provinces was evaluated and analyzed by comparison.[24]

China has not done well in the disclosure of budget information, and some scholars time after time wrote articles criticizing that the size of government was too large and people were refused knowledge of the government's real fiscal revenues and expenditures. In such a context, the performance of budgetary supervision work was not ideal. Professor Li Wei-guang from Tianjin University of Finance and Economics once listed the specific gaps between Chinese budget information disclosure and the minimum IMF requirements. According to the specific requirements of 16 items in 3 categories from public information availability, disclosure of budgetary compilation, implementation, reporting, and

[24] Jiang Hong. Report on China's Financial Transparency — Assessment of Provincial Financial Information Disclosure (2009), Shanghai: Shanghai University of Finance and Economics Press, 2009: 5.

guarantee of truth, China's statistical result was that 13 items did not meet the requirements, 2 items partially did and 1 item generally did.[25] The truth that China's fiscal revenue information is neither available to the public nor to the deputies to the People's Congress highlights an urgent need of promoting fiscal information disclosure. In such a context, the studies are quite difficult but the meaning is rather significant. Disclosure and transparency of budget information is actually the core of budgetary supervision.

4. Analysis from the Perspective of Practical Supervision of Provincial People's Congress and the System Plight

In recent years, the provinces in China have made unprecedented achievements in making laws on budgetary supervision and a large number of laws and regulations have had good results. By the end of 2006, all the provincial People's Congress throughout the country have made decrees, decisions, and regulations on strengthening examination and supervision of budgetary review, gradually improving the legal system of budgetary supervision by local People's Congress. But provincial budgetary supervision encountered a lot of substantive problems and consequently supervision basically remains on the procedural level. Especially in preliminary examination, intervention of the People's Congress is inadequate without enough time for the work of preliminary examination, and it is difficult to exercise the power to amend the draft budget.

The Budget Law in China does not provide the People's Congress and the deputies the right to amend the draft budget. In recent years in some provinces, the deputies to the People's Congress are provided with the power to amend budgets by the People's Congress in the decrees, decisions, or regulations on budgetary supervision, but they need further standardization in the system. Innovations made by the provincial People's Congress in China in the power of amending draft budget shares some common characteristics. In most provinces, the related terms are too simple and the substantive and procedural contents are neither specific nor clear, thus increasing uncertainty of actual operation. In some provinces,

[25] Li Wei-guang. Chinese Tax: Blood of Morality should Flow. *South Wind*, 2010, (2).

the right to amend is even just mentioned without any specific regulations on the proposal of the amendment.

The team led by Professor Zhao Wen in Shanghai municipal People's Congress stated in the report, "Researches into Budgetary Examination and Supervision of Local People's Congress," that at present, the preliminary examination of budget could not really form a check and balance system against the government's power of budget by the People's Congress in terms of time, content, and procedure. Therefore it is recommended to grant the People's Congress the power of approving changes of major financial projects, the power to amend draft budget and to punish illegal activities, expanding coverage of the budgets, detailing compilation of budget, ensuring enough time to compile and examine the budgets and establishing an independent budgetary compilation committee and having audit agencies independent from the government.[26]

5. Analysis from the Perspective of the Relationship Between Development of National Legal System and Local Finance

In China, the political system is a center-dominated system while the central and local fiscal system is fully decentralized. Throughout the 1980s, China's fiscal system had undergone many important changes, transferring from a concentrated budgetary revenue allocation system fully controlled by the central government into relatively decentralized institutional arrangements. Provincial fiscal expenditures keep nearly 70% of the total national fiscal expenditures since over a decade. The provincial People's Congress of all provinces have the legislative power in terms of budgetary supervision, and the systems that are relatively perfect and practical in implementation have positive impacts on economic and social development of the province, thus evolving competition between the provinces to a certain extent. Professor Christine P. Wong (Huang Pei-hua) from the University of Washington believed that the local governments have no autonomy or freedom in normal budgets but in sharp contrast, they almost have all of the autonomy in non-budgetary funds. Besides, they have

[26] Zhao Wen. *Concise Reading of Budget Examination and Supervision of Local People's Congress*, Shanghai: Fudan University Press, 2008: 179–201.

sufficient incentive to have more funds excluded from the budgets as the central government could take over their income.[27] This implies that it is very important to supervise local finance as there are few such countries in the world as China where most of the revenues are finally directly invested in the development of economy, which indeed is the most important motivation to reform the budgetary system and is also the biggest exerting point of people's concern for national development trends.

Other American professors such as Wildavsky, Irene Rubin and Jonathan Kahn have made a lot of researches into budgetary democracy from the perspective of the American history of public budgetary system reform, focusing on the reform of budgetary process and budgetary authority. Although their researches do not directly touch upon the budgetary supervision system in China, the political exploration in the budgetary process, researches of the history of American local budgetary reform in the Progressive Era and the political game between American executive and legislative in the budgetary process are useful and valuable reference for researches on the Chinese corresponding system.

Section 3. Research Methods and Basic Outline

Budgetary supervision is a constitutional power of the People's Congress at all levels. Budgetary examination and supervision of the People's Congress should be made in accordance with the laws. Currently, the legal system of the budgetary supervision of the National People's Congress is still not complete, making it difficult for the People's Congress at all levels and the standing committee to effectively exercise their powers. Budgetary supervision of the local People's Congress and standing committee are just generally stated in The Constitution, the Local Organization Law and the Budget Law and many important issues are not addressed in corresponding laws and regulations. Furthermore, the Budget Law is not mature as it was enacted before the reform of departmental budgets. Regulation on the Implementation of the Budget Law of the State Council is not very practical.

---

[27] Huang Pei-hua. *China: National Development and Local Finance*, Beijing: CITIC Publishing House, 2003: 34.

Many laws are just partially completed without further clear definitions and provisions. Therefore, the author has carried out studies on this proposition from a constitutional point of view, finding some issues existing in the process of budgetary supervision by the provincial People's Congress based on legal analyses and further exploring the approach to reasonably allocate the laws and the supervision powers to solve the problems. Researches on the provincial People's Congress budgetary supervision system must touch constitutional democracy starting from researches on budgetary democracy with attempts to enrich the academic exploration in the constitutional discipline. It should evaluate provincial People's Congress budgetary supervision system in China from entities and procedures, analyze the causes, find solutions to the problems, and make exploration in the issue of democratic structures, and the system to be solved for the sake of substantial budgetary supervision and at the same time pay attention to the cases and provide feasible and empirical discussion of knowledge for promotion of democracy in budgetary supervision and in the legal system in modern China based on the performance of the budgetary supervision system in practice. Researches made by other scholars from various perspectives in other disciplines must be considered as a reference.

Some good directions are selected in the studies made by scholars on the budgetary supervision of provincial People's Congress. Some scholars demonstrate the position of budgetary supervision on the work of People's Congress from the perspective of the constitutional analysis and the constitutional significance of budgetary supervision authority of the People's Congress. Political researchers study the nature of public budget and make empirical researches on specific budgetary democracy of provincial People's Congress from the angle of the game between public powers and civil rights, providing the basis for the author's empirical analysis.

The basis of budgetary supervision relies on the access to all budget information. Researchers in public management compare the situations of budget information disclosure at the provincial level, offering the author a good thinking about the fundamental parts of the researches on budgetary supervision. In addition, some scholars study the budgetary supervision system itself, which is also a field to be studied deeply by the author, pointing out the absence of the system in the process of budgetary supervision. The researches made by some foreign scholars from the relationship between development of national laws and local public finance also inspire the author's relative macro thinking and the idea of comparative studies. Therefore, the author attempts to explore the problems existing in provincial People's Congress budgetary supervision and the solutions based on the results of these studies, expecting to find solutions from the allocation of powers.

1. Research Methods

The main perspective of this topic under discussion is the Constitutional law with focus on analysis of power control, checks and balances, and procedures. The proposition of budgetary supervision needs close attention to the basic issues and judgments in economics and politics, but the perspective of legal theory determines that more fields should be studied, from protecting and promoting of human rights and limiting government authorities for solutions to the problems existing in the supervision system, especially the critical issues of power control during the implementation of the systems.

1. *Normative analytical method.* There is a big blank in the discussion of China's grassroots (especially provincial) budgetary supervision system since the system construction in this area is weak and practice is quite disorderly. It is necessary to combine the relevant disciplines and clarify the superior concept of the whole system in theory, thus acting as great positive guidance for establishment and improvement of relevant laws and regulations. In particular, it is quite necessary to define clearly the nature, boundaries, and classification of many powers. The supervision of the budgetary system is external manifestation of a system with the link between the public finance and the constitutional state at the core, in particular, the constitutional principle. It is an issue that cannot be fully and clearly explained by scholars in the fields of public finance and economics although researches in other disciplines are made earlier than those in law.

2. *Empirical research method.* Constitutional studies on the budgetary supervision system mainly involve rationality of the political structure and

the final results of the studies guide the system in practice at the operational level. The differences between the empirical description and summary of regional development are particularly important for the studies of provincial system. The legal text of various provinces will be analyzed by comparison, and local laws and regulations on compilation and supervision of the budgets at the provincial level are collected with emphases on government budget reports, reports on implementation of budget, relevant provisions of the provincial People's Congress and standing committee and reports of special investigations. Finding regular issues from broad information can break the usual logic of derivation from theory to the system, making recommendations for reform more credible.

3. *Historical research method.* Studies on the history can help identify the causes and the results of evolution of the system. Exploration in the political background of the government budgetary systems in different stages of economic and social development is a necessary condition of studying the contradictions and dilemmas of the present system. Self-breakthrough or improvement of a system after coming to a certain stage of development is actually based on a summary of the history of the system. Constitution is a subject in which the political life of each stage of the history is particularly summarized, and the characteristics of development of different political systems are compared based on historical studies, and finally a system model for the current situation is summarized. Evolution of budgetary supervision system is closely linked with adjustment of national financial systems and with the government goal of building public finance and priorities of fiscal reform. Thus, the country's major economic policy changes, and the ideas of development of the government financial system at different stages need to be particularly studied.

4. *Comparative study method.* Although comparison of the budgetary examination and supervision systems of the local and central governments of the major developed countries in the world is not the main methodology of studies since the scope of the researches is the local government in China, advantages of the system in major countries in the west can be drawn on as the budgetary supervision system in China is immature. Significant differences in the system between various provinces are

worthy of comparison and studies, thus helping figure out the solutions to the legal system from the aspects of Chinese characteristic.

5. *Interdisciplinary study method.* As budgetary supervision is a complex field of the features of interdisciplinary research, it is necessary to grasp and compare the principles of the budget in economics and politics. Legal research is characterized by sometimes showing a normative system of technical and applied research. In modern state public finance is not only the national economic base of various activities but also the basic means to protect citizens' property rights and human rights and thus studies on such a system of dual character need fully understanding of theoretical principles and norms about the system in different disciplines.

2. Research Framework

The book consists of the introduction and six chapters.

The introduction puts forth the background and value of the topic under discussion and further analyzes its theoretical basis and expects the theoretical issues to be resolved. It starts from interdisciplinary perspectives and makes a brief literature review and elaborates the research outline and methodology in the end.

Chapter 1 focuses on the general theory of budgetary supervision of the People's Congress. The first section makes theoretical analysis of the budgetary supervision — its theoretical basis and constitutional and political functions. After conducting some analysis on the principles and theories of several disciplines, this section summarizes the connotations, nature and features of the power of budgetary supervision from the perspective of the Constitution. The second section explores the constitutional and political significance of the mechanism of budgetary supervision. Proceeding from the constitutional and political logic between the protection of citizen's basic rights and budgetary supervision, it further explores the issue of local government's participation of democratic theoretical construction and practical regulation-making. The third section mainly explores the basic principle of budgetary supervision.

Chapter 2 discusses the regulation of budgetary supervision by the People's Congress at the provincial level. The first section summarizes the development of its supervision power, regulations and the legislative foundation of its legal construction. The second section introduces the origin of the supervision regulation from a general perspective. Although the province in China has the legislative power, it has to be guided by the regulations and laws made by the central government. The third section introduces the main content and procedure of supervision.

Chapter 3 concentrates on the problems during the supervision and their reasons. The biggest problem in supervision is that it can hardly be conducted with real effects. The first section analyzes the problem of the rules of budgetary supervision. The second section mainly dwells on the problem of insufficient revelation of budget information and discusses the reason from different angles. The third section analyzes the insubstantial budgetary supervision from the perspectives of supervision power, deficiency of legislative guarantee, and limitation of political practices with some case studies on the regulations in Shanghai, as well as Guangdong and Gansu provinces.

Chapter 4 is on the reasonable allocation of budgetary supervision power. Budgetary supervision is a political process where all the powers participating in the supervision should be well-balanced and reasonably-allocated, which is a necessary precondition for the improvement of the regulation of budgetary supervision. The second section explores the power of supervision during this process and mainly discusses the amendment of the draft budget and the standardization and specification of the power of budgetary supervision in order to make it play the central role in the supervision process. The third section explores reasonable limitation of the budgetary supervision power by the People's Congress.

Chapter 5 is on the guarantee of the disclosure of budget information. The first section analyzes the status quo of the disclosure of budget information and its legal problems accordingly, and then summarizes the problems arising from the lack of legal construction on the right to know the budget information. The second section puts forth some suggestions to improve the disclosure system of budget information from the perspectives of legal guarantee and specific disclosure principles.

Chapter 6 dwells on the improvement of the budgetary supervision procedure. The first section puts forth the suggestion on the general regulation of reinforcing the supervision in the whole process. The second section discusses the improvement and standardization in the budget. The third section explores the improvement of supervision during the budgetary implementation, trying to avoid insubstantial supervising power in the budgetary supervision process.

The final Conclusion summarizes the ways to solve the problems of budgetary supervision by the People's Congress at the provincial level and points out some areas that are left uncovered for further research.

Chapter 1

General Theory of Budgetary Supervision of the People's Congress

The British bourgeois aristocracy in 1215 forced the king to sign the Magna Carta, putting it as a rule that the King could collect tax unless he was allowed by the nobility. With continuous struggles, the bourgeoisie made more victory in the provisions that the King was not free to collect and use tax. Furthermore, the revenues of tax and the expenditures of budget had to be approved by the Parliament with an annual allocation of revenues and expenditures which should be approved and supervised by the Parliament. As the basis and core of the modern state of financial systems, the budgetary system is naturally associated with basic values of democracy, the laws, and rights. Except life, property delivery is the greatest sacrifice the citizens make to the society and government representatives achieve publicity of the public finance on behalf of the civil society and meet public benefits.

However, for good governance of the nation, fiscal factors have to be taken into consideration while the boundaries of powers and rights is set and organizational form and state structure are designed and adjusted by the Constitution makers. As the public finance must be dependent on people through mechanisms such as taxes and bonds, excessive tax or loss of bonds credits will directly endanger political stability and safety of the government. Shortage of financial resources is always a natural obstacle to restricting the government powers. Savings and efficient use of financial resources are always the issues that must be considered by the rational Constitution makers.[1]

[1] Zhou Gang-zhi. *On Public Finance and Constitutional State — As a Theoretical Preamble of Financial Constitution*, Beijing: Peking University Press, 2005: 33–34.

Government budgetary supervision of the representative who represents the civil society is the base of budgetary democracy. In a budgetary democratic system, the whole process of budgetary supervision including compilation, examination, approval and adjustment should reflect people's participation and decision-making. On the one hand, budgetary democracy is reflected by parliamentary examination, approval, and supervision of budget; on the other hand, in addition to representative bodies' power to take part in budgetary process, the people should also have other channels to participate in and supervise the budget, for example, gaining information and feedback through media such as newspapers and television network. At present, in China, the government budgetary supervision system consists of legislative, executive, and judicial organs of state supervision and a variety of social supervision through various channels has formed. However, other forms of supervision should be absorbed in the legislative process and finally have it come into legal effect by supervision of the People's Congress.

In this book, for a better study of the budgetary supervision system problem, the legal scope of budgetary supervision must be defined at first, namely the aspects of budgetary supervision. As for this question, domestic scholars have different opinions — some scholars argue that budgetary supervision starts from the implementation of budget and excludes approving or amending draft budget and others believe that the scope of supervision should include the draft budget approval, amendment, and implementation of budget. This is a premise of the study and it must be clearly defined. The author believes that budgetary supervision is a very special power of the representative bodies. Seen from parliament history, when early parliament appeared, it was authorized to supervise government finances from the beginning, rather than intermediate and afterwards supervision as budgetary supervision of the representative bodies is a process of fully participating in decision-making and exercising of supervision powers, including budgetary compilation, examination, approval and implementation, and adjustment or change of budget. The legal basis of supervision and the measures of improvement can be explored as long as the legal scope of budgetary supervision has been defined.

Section 1. Theoretical Analysis of Budgetary Supervision

1. Theoretical Basis for Budgetary Supervision

1. *Analysis of the constitutional relationship between public finance and representative system.* Representative system, the basis of the system of modern constitutional state, is the key to the implementation of the Constitution. Budgetary supervisory power of the representatives is a key system setting of the principle of separation of constitutional powers. As a result, budgetary supervision involves a constitutional issue — the relationship between legislative and executive powers. The taxpayers are the providers of public budget revenue sources and also the beneficiaries of public budget expenditures. They are surely most associated with the public finance as their living are most directly tied with the public finance and thus they should take part in and supervision of the public budgets.

The fundamental rights of citizens, such as the right to participate, right to know, and right to supervise can be realized only in the process of supervision. To prevent those who implement the budget from having too many powers and taxpayers' rights from being infringed due to lack of budget information and non-transparency in the procedure, systematic channels must be established to allow taxpayers to participate in public budgetary supervision and the best systematic channel is the budgetary supervision system of the People's Congress. As the People's Congress is a representative body of the citizens and has constitutional power of budgetary supervision and holds the power of public finance through its internal organs, its supervisory role in the whole process of public budget cannot be taken or replaced by any other institutions.

Since the parliamentary power of examination and approval of the budget is introduced in a country's constitutional system and becomes an integral part of the government on the financial system, economic measures and actions of the government must be approved by the Parliament. The government's affairs will be directly supervised by the voters for the sake of reasonable control and final protection of people's rights by checks and balances of separation of powers.[2] As Marx said, strong government and heavy taxes are the same concept. Unrestricted

[2] Zhu Kong-wu. *On Financial Constitutionalism*, Beijing: Law Press, 2006: 125.

public powers are inevitably linked with unrestricted financial power. Therefore, to restrict the government's unrestricted public power, its financial power should be restricted firstly. In essence, control of public financial power is the key to restrict state power and the constitutional system.

Control of public finance is not only the core of the checks and balances system of state power but also the base of protecting citizens' fundamental rights such as property and personal rights. The nature of public finance is parliamentary centralism. Government authority to handle financial affairs must be based on the Parliament's resolutions and laws. The budget approved by the Parliament and the related documents that constrain financial activities of the government are laws in the country and must be fully and exactly abided by the government. All collection of tax and charges without permission of the Parliament or under the pretext of the privileges or benefits of government heads or departments and financial behaviors beyond Parliamentary permission are illegal.[3]

The public budget represents a sort of principal–agency relationship which has very special characteristic of complicated levels of commission. A property owner entrusts the property to a manager who manages the property for the sake of the owner and has partial property managed by a subordinate manager, thus creating multiple levels of principal–agent relationship. The longer the chain of the principal–agent is, the more severe information asymmetry will be and the more uncertain the principal–agent relationship will become. The agent may bring damage to the public interests in pursuit of departmental or individual interests. The ambiguity of the public interest will also lead the owner to have a virtual position and cause loss and waste of public budgetary allocation, which fails to reflect the preferences of the public interests and even leads to serious problems such as rent-seeking and the issue of insider control.

In public choice theory, it is believed that the government is a collection of economic activities of the individuals who have different specific

---

[3] Li Wei-guang. The Constitutional Thinking of the Public Finances. *Strategy and Management*, 2002, (3): 21.

interests and pursue maximal benefits. The government changes individual's private choice into public choice during the political process, in which the government agencies and officials may abuse public power, seek private interests, and operate inefficiently. Therefore, it is necessary to strengthen the supervision over the decision-makers. In case the public interests conflict with the departmental interests, it will be very necessary for the public society to constrain and supervise the government departments through the selected representative institutions.[4] The process from public budgetary compilation up to implementation is a process of selection and confirmation of public interests, which needs broad public participation and full transparency of budget information. Studies in public choice theory show that bureaucrats tend to conceal inefficient administrative action by simplifying financial information. Without disclosure of current expenditures and future policies, it seems that the voters will be fiscally illusive and unaware of a great amount of financial waste.[5]

The government's fiscal power is the basis of effective governmental activities, but on the other hand, the private property rights of the citizens can be seriously damaged if the government and its public officers abuse such a power. Seen from opportunism of the managers, the officials or managers who control and manage public items seem to damage the interests of the client, that is to say the public interest. The government administrative organs submit their budget plans to the legislative for approval and after that they usually have freedom in implementation of the budgets such as controlling the power to approve the projects, to transfer, deliver, and use the funds. The administrative organs and their officials may go astray from the expected objectives of the principal, that is to say, damaging the public interests in the pursuit of maximizing their own interests.[6] So when the powers of budgetary compilation and implementation are given to the government, at the same time a complete system must be

---

[4] Li Chuan-xi. Assessment of theory of Public Choice and the Doctrine of Separation of Constitutional Powers and Evaluation on the Improvement of Budget Supervision System in China. *Theory and Reform*, 2003, (6).

[5] He Jun-zhi. Theoretical Origins and International Practice of Budget Transparency. *Institute of National Public Administration*, 2008, (2): 91.

[6] Jiang Long. Theoretical Origins of Financial Supervision in Public Finance. *Financial Research*, 2001, (11): 15.

established so that the representative body has the power to examine and approve the budgets. Such an approval system is not only the core of mutual restraint of constitutional state powers but also the foundation of establishment of a democratic financial model.

Although at present local governments in China are exposed to a financial risk as the result of considerable debts, it is rather the local governments' freedom to spend money without control that is more worrisome than the debts. What puts the Chinese financial state are It is the deficiencies in the fiscal supervision system in the transitional period that puts the Chinese financial state in a very difficult situation. The local public finance in many regions just reflects personal wills of some heads of the Party or the government, and a large number of funds are used for the political achievement projects of the governments in various terms, from large airports and power plants to luxury office buildings, hotels, and amusement parks. Such a financial decision-making system without supervision is bound to bring a heavy tax burden.

The national audit office audited and investigated the management of finances in 2008 and in January to June of 2009 in 17 provinces and autonomous regions and found problems in compilation of the budgets, revenue collection and management, and financial resources management that were not implemented in a standard or strict way. In four provinces and autonomous regions, the funds promised by the treasury department were not all included in their budgets for 2009 with 36.352 billion Yuan of central special transfer funds were excluded. In order to attract investment, 7 provincial and 59 local governments below the provincial level and development zones made policies without permission in tax reduction, tax rebating, or returning the land transfer fees in the name of government premium of financial subsidies involving an amount of 12.573 billion Yuan.

Four provincial and 10 local governments below the provincial level and development zones returned 463 million Yuan of income tax to more than 20,000 top executives in business in the name of housing subsidies, car subsidies, and talent rewards. In 12 provinces and 26 counties, 79.416 billion Yuan of non-tax revenue including land transfer fees and compensation fees for mineral resources that should have been collected was not collected, in which land sale income was 94.76%. In 17 provinces and autonomous regions, 62.538 billion Yuan of non-tax income that was collected was not paid on time into the treasury for budgetary management as required and were kept in interim accounts or non-budgetary accounts of the departments of tax collection. In 17 provinces and autonomous regions, except treasury deposit accounts of the financial departments, 1197 accounts were opened in commercial banks, in which 920 more than 50 per province in average.[7]

This mode of financial operation results from China's highly centralized political system and deficiencies in the system will encourage local governments and their officials to abuse power. To solve the various problems existing in China's public finance system and the practice of public finance, analyses and explorations made at the level of financial and monetary policies in the country are not enough. The problems of expansion of government financial power and lack of control can only be solved at the level of constitutionalism by constraining government financial power through legal reforms.[8]

2. *The constitutional logic of the principles of financial democracy.* The supervision of the government budget by the People's Congress is just a means of achieving financial democracy. The fundamental objective of financial democracy is to provide the people the right of disposition of public finances consisting of tax paid by themselves, and the right of disposition surely refers to the most important rights such as the right of making decision and the right of supervision, collectively called the right to supervise. Theoretical basis of financial democracy is the idea of sovereignty that belongs to the people. According to the concept of democracy, what financial democracy requires is that the people exercise the right of making decisions in major national financial issues through certain procedures and methods in accordance with the laws. The direct requirements are that significant financial issues must be approved by representative agencies or regulated by the laws made by them. Without parliamentary resolutions or authorization by the laws, revenues or

---

[7]Auditing Results of Financial Management in 17 Provinces and Municipalities, State Audit Bureau. 2010, (12).

[8]Zhou Gang-zhi. *On Public Finance and Constitutional State — As a Theoretical Preamble of Financial Constitution*, Beijing: Peking University Press, 2005: 131.

expenditures are likely to be accused of violating the people's will. Thus, the meaning of democracy is to achieve people's self-management and autonomous decision-making and thereby advance the realization and guarantee of their rights.[9]

What financial democracy reflects is the idea of sovereignty belonging to the people in the Constitution. Financial democracy demands that giving people a wide range of power of supervision over financial matters and requiring the financial behavior of decision-making, the process and the result of implementation are open and transparent.[10] Public finance can be truly democratic only if it is democratic in the process. Budgetary supervision is the substantive implementation of a system in the process of democratic supervision over public finance by the representative agencies on behalf of civil society. Based on the principle of democratic centralism, the People's Congress forms and supervises the government. Budgetary supervision is the most important and basic supervision over the government by the People's Congress.

In the planned economy supervision has only financial significance without political significance and it can help the government improve only its financial management system. However, with the state finance turning into the form of tax, budgetary supervision of the People's Congress is of full political significance. As in the supervision, the People's Congress must represent the public interests of the citizens who directly created taxes.[11] Therefore, only when the representative agencies participate in the budgetary process for supervision on behalf of the interests of all citizens, the tax-payers, public finance will be democratic substantively.

Since the 1980s, many standing committees of the People's Congress at the provincial level began to make normative documents on budgetary supervision, marking the beginning of the era of exercise of the powers of budgetary supervision at the local level in a standard and democratic

---

[9] Liu Jian-wen. Constitutionalism and Chinese Financial Democracy. *Tax Research*, 2008, (4): 4.

[10] *Ibid.*

[11] Lin Shang-li. Financial Basis of Democratic Centralism — An Analysis of Chinese National Construction. *Social Sciences*, 2006, (11): 39.

way. With increase in financial opportunities for the local government by China's reform and opening up, especially introduction of tax-sharing system, local governments at all levels in China have more financial freedom, and a lot of financial administration actually comes from too much government discretion rather than public interests. The process of decision-making, implementation, supervision, control, and performance evaluation of financial expenditures is not ensured by a democratic system, so fiscal deficit grows at the same pace as economy does in which local governments, in particular the provincial governments, have the greatest responsibility, as the provincial governments are the only local governments with legislative powers and at the same time are the hub of the political system in China. Provincial People's Congress must intensify supervision and management of public finance from a legal point of view to make the system operational and truly protect the public interests.

The first requirement of budgetary democracy is democracy of budgetary decisions, which means that decision-making of all the activities involving the budget must be made through democratic procedures to ensure the people to be the masters of the country and reflect the interests and aspirations of the people. In China, budgetary activities are actually dominated by the government. It would emphasize control of the government while neglect parliamentary sovereignty and democratic supervision over the budget.

First, democracy of budgetary decision-making is marked by the practice that the representative agencies should make decisions and impose supervision in the activities of budgetary compilation. Secondly, it is marked by the power of budgetary examination and approval of the representative agencies. Democracy is always based on publicity of democratic affairs, and budgetary democracy is surely based on openness of budgetary affairs. Openness of budgetary affairs refers to full disclosure of all information except state secrets in the whole process of budget including compilation and implementation. Budgetary supervision aims to reflect the people's will in budgetary decisions. Although the People's Congress is given the power of budgetary supervision on behalf of the public in accordance with the laws, to truly supervise government public budget, representatives of the people still have to rely on the citizens and other agencies in supporting supervision. Public opinion supervision and social supervision should be paid attention to as it is a legitimate way of participation in management of budgetary affairs for the people. With openness of budget, the media and the people will be concerned more about the budget, and their supervision will help the state power organs and representatives of the people to find the problems in time.

3. *Constitutional functions of financial budget.* In a modern nation, public finance is not only a prerequisite of state power but also a material means of regulating and restricting the state powers. For termination of authoritarian rule, the first thing is to establish a parliament to control the taxation system on behalf of the interests of the taxpayers. Public finance constructed by the representative is of constitutional function that is irreplaceable and cannot be ignored. Public finance can commonly explain the emergence of theory of sovereignty belonging to the people: as the material basis of the existence and operation of a nation-state is provided by the people through taxes and consequently it should be used for and limited by the people.

In fact, public finance contains a sort of social contract relationship between the taxpayer and the state.[12] Financial budget is not only the economic premise of normal operation of a state power but also an important political means to limit state power. On the one hand, financial budget provides the government the material basis and acknowledges legitimacy of government position and is the starting point of all political instruments and on the other, control of government budget expenditures is a fundamental means to prevent the government from corruption and abusing public powers. Through such a supervision system, the government can always operate under the supervision of the people and this reflects the important role of citizens in the framing and implementation of the budget.

The nature of financial affairs in constitutionalism is an interaction of the property rights of the citizens and the financial powers of the government. In the history of constitutionalism, it is financial power that led to

[12] Wei Jian-guo. *Formation of Constitutional System and Rise of Modern Britain*, Beijing: Law Press, 2006: 16.

the emergence and development of constitutionalism and is also the basic guarantee of operation of constitutionalism. On the one hand, the governments at various levels in a state obtain public finance from the civil society in accordance with the laws and it is the most fundamental way of recognizing state power by the people; on the other hand, coordination of fiscal relations in dealing with the relationship between the central and local governments in the nation is a basic form of operation of the national constitutionalism. Public finance functions in the way of transfer payments between the governments at various levels and such a fiscal relation between the governments can only be effectively controlled with very strict laws on financial budget in the light of fairness and efficiency.

If public finance is under people's supervision, such a budgetary system would be very conducive to establishing a truly limited government. The reality is that in China, a large part of public finance in the governments at various levels is used to develop the economy, which is abnormal. In such a disorderly state, the government cannot be well-supervised within the framework of constitutionalism, which hastens corruption at various levels, thus hindering social and economic development to a large extent and even causing social instability. Unlimited governments in which public financial budgets are not effectively supervised will conversely impose more financial burden on the people.

To achieve the constitutionalism goal of separation of civil society and politics, the only way is to have the power of supervision over public financial budget firmly controlled by the people and their representative agencies. The objective of public finance is to control the financial powers of a state. With expansion and strengthening of government functions in modern society, the scale, form, and performance of governmental budgets of revenues and expenditures should be controlled by representative agencies at any moment. Only when the power of budgetary supervision of the People's Congress is strengthened in a variety of ways, can the civil society firmly constrain the powerful governments, and further prevent them from behaviors against the public interests and ensure the fundamental rights of the citizens.

2. Broad Meaning of Budgetary Supervision

As a public power of the representative agencies, the scope of budgetary supervision in the laws is the first major issue to be studied at the theoretical level. It will affect how the provincial People's Congress can be involved in budgetary supervision and make judgment. The Parliament's power of budgetary supervision is one of the most important powers of the state legislative for supervision over financial behaviors of state organs. Budgetary supervision is not just supervision after decisions have been made but is also the power of making decisions. The People's Congress must participate in the process of supervision and decision-making. The special budgetary supervision department of the People's Congress and the government budgetary compilation departments should even work together at the very beginning of budgetary compilation to save the costs of coordination.

In studying the supervision of government behaviors by the People's Congress, Professor Cai Ding-jian divided the financial supervision of the People's Congress into three types: Examination and approval of plans and budgets, supervision over implementation of budget, and examination and approval of partial change of the budget in the process of implementation. The examination and approval of plans and budgets can be said to be macro supervision in advance and is one of the most important kinds of supervision of the People's Congress over government behaviors to control all government activities, since funds are the foundation of all government activities.[13]

Supervision itself is nothing more than a constraint of power. Supervision of state administrative agencies by state power organs should contain effective control of all government administrative acts within the scope set by the Constitution and the laws. It is probably very difficult to clearly differentiate between the decision-making power and the power of supervision in certain aspects. Once the power of supervision becomes concrete, it will inevitably contain a decision-making power, which is the main content of the power of supervision itself. For

[13] Cai Ding-jian. *The People's Congress System in China* (Fourth Edition), Beijing: Law Press, 2003: 376.

instance, supervision of the implementation of budget by the standing committee of the People's Congress is mainly presented as a decision-making power especially when there are adjustments or changes in the process of implementation of the budget. If deviation occurs in the process of budgetary implementation the People's Congress or its standing committee is entitled to take action after strict examination in accordance with the laws.

Once the so-called power of supervision becomes concrete, it will turn into a decision-making power in specific matters while the decision-making power is reflected in the whole process of supervision and so it is difficult to totally differentiate between them.[14] Thus the decision-making power of the budget is within the scope of the power of budgetary supervision. It is a very important theoretical premise. If the People's Congress cannot take part in the amendments to the draft budget before or during a formal meeting, it could be considered that substantive power of supervision of the People's Congress is non-existent. According to the Constitution, the People's Congress and its standing committee is entitled to the power of making decision in major issues, and the examination and approval of the budget is just one of the approaches of exercising such a power by the People's Congress.

In this book, budgetary supervision is discussed in a broad sense. The two types of powers that the People's Congress is entitled to by the Constitution are examination and approval of budget and the power of amendment to draft budget. The local People's Congress highlights the supervision of the budget in three areas: The first is examination of the draft budget, focusing on reasonable allocation of financial resources and balance of the revenues and expenditures; the second is supervision over implementation of the budget, focusing on strict control of financial funds by examination, approval, and management of budget and promoting and deepening departmental budget reforms in treasury collection, government procurement, and separation of revenues and expenditures; the third is special investigation for important sectors and major projects, focusing on performance evaluation, promoting strict implementation of financial

---

[14] Li Lan-Ying, Liu Hui. System Defects of China's People's Congress Budget Supervision. *Journal of Central University of Finance and Economics*, 2006, (12): 17–18.

laws and regulations, strengthening internal controls, and preventing misappropriation of funds, corruption, and wastage.[15]

Comprehensive budgetary supervision is the basis of good supervision. According to the second paragraph of Article 11, Regulation for the Implementation of the Budget Law, the local budgetary revenues as mentioned in the first paragraph of Article 20 of the Budget Law refers to the revenues that are brought into the local budgets and that are not shared by the central government according to the tax-sharing system between the central and local governments, including revenues at the local levels and revenues refunded or subsidized to the local governments by the central government. It shows that effectiveness of the budgetary supervision has been extended to the central transfer payments to provincial governments in the laws. As the funds cannot be included in provincial budgets in specific provincial financial operations, it would be difficult for the provincial People's Congress to impose effective supervision over this part of the funds.

"Guiding Opinions on Local Government Report to the People's Congress on Financial Budgets, Draft Final Accounts, and Implementation of Budget" issued by the Ministry of Finance in 2005 put it as a regulation that the government, in accordance with the Budget Law, should report to the People's Congress the implementation of budget in the first half of the current year and the draft budget for the next year and to the standing committee of the People's Congress on the final accounts of the previous year, implementation of budget in months, and budgetary adjustments. The reports should be consistent with the relevant requirements of examination, approval, and supervision. The reports should consist of two parts, text and statement. The text should include the main items of revenues and expenditures and main financial work, in particular, explanations for the important items of expenditures, items of superior transfer payments, and the annual budget balance of revenues and expenditures. The statements should include the report of main class-level subjects according to Items of Government Budget Revenues and Expenditures made by the Ministry of Finance.

---

[15] Zhao Wen. Research Reports on Local People's Congress Budget Examination and Supervision. *Condensed Reading of Local People's Congress Budget Examination and Supervision*, Shanghai: Fudan University Press, 2008: 217–218.

In 2006, the Ministry of Finance issued supplementary notes on local government's report to the People's Congress on financial draft budget, draft final accounts, and implementation of the budget. The aim of the supplementary notes is just to emphasize that the tax return and subsidies for the local governments should be fully included in the budget of the government. Meanwhile, the budget of the government should reflect tax return and lower subsidies for the subordinates. Notice on Compilation of 2007 Central and Local Budgets of the State Council once again clearly requires the provincial governments to have income of central government tax refunded and subsidies fully included in the total provincial budget and meanwhile provide the amount of tax return and subsidies to the subordinate governments in the budget. It reflects the recognition of the State Council on comprehensiveness of local government budgetary compilation and the concern for this work.

The supplementary notice issued in 2006 is flexible as it requires taking specific measures for implementation to ensure that the contents of the financial draft budget, draft final accounts, and implementation of budget to be supervised by the People's Congress are complete and accurate. But in many places, the incomes refunded or subsidized by the central government are not included in the local budget, so it is difficult for the local People's Congress to supervise.[16] Although the State Council has made rather strict special provisions on comprehensive budgetary compilation, the national audit bureau found some problems in its audit of provincial financial management. The results of the audits and investigations into financial budget management in 18 provinces and autonomous regions made by the national audit bureau in July 2009 show that in some regions, budgetary compilation of special subsidies from superior governments is incomplete.

In the selected 13 provinces, 212.771 billion Yuan of special subsidies from the central government was not included in the budget of the government for 2007, equal to 61.74% of 344.634 billion Yuan of central special subsidies in the last year. In 6 provinces, the central special

[16] *China Development Research Foundation. Public Budgets Reading*, Beijing: China Development Press, 2008: 90–91.

subsidies were not included in the budget of the government at all.[17] The results of the audits and investigations into financial budget management in 17 provinces and autonomous regions made by the national audit bureau in June 2010 show that in 4 provinces and autonomous regions, the statement of central special transfer payments budget is incomplete. To make local budget compilation complete, the Ministry of Finance began to inform the expected number of special transfer payments from the central government from the end of 2008, and required the local governments to accordingly compile and report budgets. Audit investigations show that in 4 provinces, autonomous regions, and municipalities, although management and use of central special transfer payments were in line with national requirements, the foreseen number informed by the Ministry of Finance was not completely included in the budget for 2009 with exclusion of 36.352 billion Yuan of central special transfer payments.[18]

Budgetary supervision enables the People's Congress to take part in the political process of budgetary allocation and thus becomes a very important institution in operation of the powers. Budgetary supervision is comprehensive and complete in the whole process and it is the legal responsibility of the People's Congress. Financial democracy is a process of interaction of powers between the government, the parliament, and the society around rational allocation of financial resources with effective control of the state treasury by a representative of Parliament, aiming to meet the fundamental requirements of sovereignty of the taxpayer and achieve the goal of restricting the government dominance in public finance on their own will.[19] Budgetary democracy is an important symbol of legitimacy of the government after successful transformation from a planned economy to a market economy and society of rule of law. Budgetary democracy can not only enhance the legitimacy of government

---

[17] Audit and Investigation Results of Tax Collection and Management of the State Taxing Departments in 16 Provinces, Autonomous Regions and Municipalities, Audit and Investigation Results of Financial Budget Management in 18 Provinces, Autonomous Regions and Municipalities. State Audit Bureau, 2009: 9.

[18] Auditing Results of Financial Management in 17 Provinces and Municipalities (No. 12 Audit Report in 2010), 2010.

[19] Xu Hong. *Financial Control and Financial Democracy*, Shanghai: Fudan University, 2006: 216.

but also help the government achieve maximization of the revenues. As the People's Congress has substantively participated in budgetary supervision, it will inevitably become a part of political power and consequently problems or even conflicts with the Party and the government will arise.

3. The Nature and Characteristics of the Power of Budgetary Supervision

Budgetary supervision is a sort of political phenomenon in a state and is carried out by the People's Congress based on the power of budgetary supervision over government behaviors. The legal basis of supervision by the People's Congress is the power of budgetary supervision. The meaning of power of budgetary supervision in law mainly refers to the power of supervision given to the representative agencies which act as organs of power in the course of compilation of the draft budget, examination and approval of the budget, and implementation of the budget. The representative agencies on behalf of the public impose financial supervision and bear public responsibility for possible failure in management. This is the basis of public financial democracy. Therefore, the power of budgetary supervision is not just examination of representative agencies in government public finance in a general sense or checking after the finalization or implementation of the budget, but is a power of financial decision-making, supervision, and control through participating in the process of the budget on behalf of the civil society. This power of the People's Congress is legally exclusive, procedural, regulatory, and mandatory, and is the exclusive national power of supervision as legislative. According to the Constitution, the power of the People's Congress is legally free of interference from other bodies and is independent from and beyond any administrative agencies and the judiciary.

Public finance system is a constitutional system design of the relationship between the state and the individuals. The system is a democratic political procedure, based on national and local budgets. The representative agencies on behalf of the citizens supervise financial activities of the government. Budgetary examination involves a constitutional issue of the relationship between legislative and executive powers. The Parliament's power of supervision in the budget proposed by the executive departments is a basic design according to the principle of separation of powers based on the Constitution in modern states. A common goal is to prevent the expansion and abuse of executive power.[20]

What a budget concerns is the process of the spending of the government's revenues and expenditure. Revenues mean the power to collect tax from the citizens, while the expenditures mainly reflect the allocation of public resources and efficiency and fairness of provision of public services. This political procedure is essentially almost all of the value of existence of a government and is the focus of both the central and the local governments at the provincial or lower level. The design of the budgetary supervision system framework of representative agencies at various levels must be operational and authoritative or it will be unable to effectively control some major issues concerning vital interests of the citizens. Representative agency is not only a legislature but also a collection of public opinions. The attribution and balancing mechanism of the budget using the executive and legislative powers is often closely related with a country's democratic development and the choice of the constitution.[21]

The organ of budgetary supervision is specific, namely the legislature. Although the People's Congress does not have executive power[22] and the nature of supervision is not a specific executive power or commanding power, supervision of the People's Congress over the only financial resources delivered by the public society will directly affect quality and efficiency of the public services provided by the government and indeed plays a decisive role in the operation and development of the state.

Budgetary supervision of the People's Congress is also obviously indirect control. As the People's Congress does not directly participate in the executive implementation and decision or directly interfere with the specific configuration of the funds of a project, effective supervision of the People's Congress over the budgets of administrative agencies is mainly based on the Constitution, the Budget Law, and other related laws. Of course, because the supervision of administrative agencies by

[20] Zhu Kong-wu. *On Financial Constitutionalism*, Beijing: Law Press, 2006: 125.

[21] Zhu Kong-wu. *On Financial Constitutionalism*, Beijing: Law Press, 2006: 261.

[22] Cai Jian. On Characteristics of Powers of Representative Agencies. *Chinese People's Congress*, 2000, (4): 20.

the legislative is based on laws, the legal effectiveness of budgetary supervision, the most authoritative type of financial supervision, is undoubtable.

1. *The subject is specific*. All the regulations on budgetary supervision made in various provinces make clear that the People's Congress and standing committee is the subject of budgetary supervision, thus endowing budgetary supervision of the provincial People's Congress with legal effectiveness. According to the laws, the power of budgetary supervision can be exercised only by the People's Congress at various levels and cannot be exercised by any other organizations or individuals. Generally speaking, the People's Congress and standing committee cannot transfer their powers of supervision to other organizations or individuals.[23] One of the main functions of the modern British Parliament is to organize, supervise, and control the national public finance.

Given that public finance is directly related to protection or deprivation of the taxpayer's freedom and property rights and protection of the rights of the whole society and the individuals, the power should be grasped by the Parliament and it cannot be transferred to other agencies, in particular, the administrative agencies cannot abuse the power of collecting tax. Independent from the government, the Parliament represents the interests of the taxpayers, reflects voice of the taxpayers and is entitled to make decisions on the major tax issues whether the government will collect tax, what tax will be collected and how to collect and is entitled to supervise the usage of the government tax.[24]

2. *Indirect supervision*. The main objective of budgetary supervision of the People's Congress is to ensure that the government financial revenues and expenditures are made public in general, namely equity and efficiency of the public services provided through public finance. But the People's Congress generally will not directly interfere in the decision-making of specific financial revenues and expenditures. The People's Congress will regularly impose strict legal supervision over government financial budget according to the existing laws and regulations and the

---

[23] Cai Ding-jian. *The People's Congress System in China* (Fourth Edition), Beijing: Law Press, 2003: 369.

[24] Wei Jian-guo. *Formation of Constitutional System and Rise of Modern Britain*, Beijing: Law Press, 2006: 118.

procedures, amend and approve the draft budget proposed by the government on the whole and supervise legality and legitimacy of implementation and adjustment of budget in the process of implementation. Indirect control of the power of budgetary supervision requires the power to be exercised in accordance with the laws, including the Constitution and special laws on budget and the specific procedures, methods and conditions to be followed in the whole process of budgetary compilation, approval, and implementation.[25]

3. *Participation in decision-making*. The principle of financial democracy requires that the People's Congress make decisions, manage, and supervise public finance. Obviously, supervision of the People's Congress over the public budget does not only include the examination of legality in the procedure but also the power of supervision over specific issues of financial revenues and expenditures. The principle of budgetary democracy requires the People's Congress to comprehensively supervise the whole process of compilation, examination, approval, and implementation of budget, thus requiring the People's Congress to participate in decision-making in public budget based on the laws and regulations. Different from the central budget, many provincial budgets involve specific financial items of revenues and expenditures and are closely concerned with the daily lives of the public. Much information can be obtained by the deputies to the People's Congress in their daily work of being representatives and in supervision. There must be various legal approaches of intervention for the deputies to the People's Congress and for the members of the standing committee of the People's Congress in the adjournment of the general assembly to make judgment and decision on the basis of information they obtain.

The local People's Congress can challenge a specific expenditure of the government; some local People's Congress and standing committee will put it as a rule in advance that government financial investment items beyond a certain amount of funds should be submitted to the People's Congress for discussion and approval. This particular mode of supervision

---

[25] Liu Jian-wen. *The Finance under Rule of Law from the Democratic Perspective*, Beijing: Peking University Press, 2006: 187.

has somewhat changed the characteristics of indirect supervision. Specific funds such as appropriations for official kindergarten, funds for provincial certified public accountants association, and funds for nine-year compulsory education in the provincial budget were even inquired at Guangdong provincial People's Congress meeting in 2004. This way, the provincial government will be very careful in the process of the compilation and implementation of public budget and always be wary of supervision by the People's Congress, thus ensuring the principle of equity and efficiency of financial funds.

Section 2. Constitutional Significance of Budgetary Supervision

1. Democratization of Budget and Supervision of Government Authority

Constitutionalism is the foundation of modern social and political balance. For China, which is a newly established modern state following the democratic system, it is primarily important to ensure the Government's self-interest and the fundamental rights of the citizens in the process of growth. Public finance, the only source of public goods, may infringe private rights on behalf of public power. Open and transparent public finance is the premise of preventing infringement and protecting the rights of the citizens. Disclosure of financial scale and use will enable the people to exactly understand how the government deals with the money and property they delivered and consequently will not doubt the motives and results of the public services provided by the government. Thus all power in China belongs to the people because the people naturally need to know how the government disposes of its financial resources in order to effectively supervise the exercise of government powers.

In recent years, various provinces in China are making steady and sustained efforts to promote openness of the budget, which reflects significant awareness created in the people. In the annual meeting of the Guangdong provincial People's Congress held in February 2010, the provincial annual budget was reviewed and voted. The financial department in Guangdong Province gave 700 deputies to the People's Congress attending the meeting a draft budget more than 613 pages, covering 116 departments at the provincial level with total budget expenditures of 469.5 billion Yuan. Some experts hold that in China, budgets are opened in a steady progressive way: in 2003, the Guangdong provincial government submitted to the People's Congress for the first time the annual budget of up to 102 departments; four years later the word "Secret" marked on the covers of the departmental budget report was removed and in 2008 all the departmental budgets were submitted to the People's Congress for examination and approval.

While promoting openness of public budgets, Guangdong is providing various facilities for examination of the budget by the People's Congress. In addition to Guangdong, other provinces and cities are also exploring ways to intensify openness of budget. After Guangdong's showing account books on the Internet, Shanghai definitely announced that it would actively explore the way, scope, and form of opening the budget, promoting sunshine finance. In the two sessions in Beijing in 2010, thin brochures containing internal data and discreet handling of these brochures were done away with. The brochures were replaced by thick books of more than 200 pages, involving 45 departments, and every delegate was given a copy and could take it home for careful reading. The sudden openness in Beijing surprised many representatives.[26]

The fulfillment of the objective of financial democracy requires appropriate division of financial powers between the legislative, executive, and judicial authorities. Generally speaking, however, the financial system and budgetary management system before the late 1980s obviously could not reach the set goal. Nevertheless, progress in budgetary supervision could be seen at that stage. Based on the financial democracy mechanism and budgetary supervision system set in the Constitution, after the reform and opening up, the People's Congress made progress in organizational structure, supervision procedures, examination methods, and local budget legislation. It is an important symbol of growth of power of supervision shown by development from principles in the Constitution to operational system arrangements. In the 1990s, local authorities at various levels

[26]Ye Qian, Wang Pan. Deputies of the Local People's Congress Actively Promote to Disclose Provincial Budget to the Whole Society. *Xinhua News Agency*, 2010, 2 (23).

obtained obvious progress. The People's Congress at all levels and its standing committee deeply took part in all aspects of budget reform, constituting the core element of the financial democracy system by exercise of the powers of legislation, decision-making, and supervision. The power of budgetary supervision of the local People's Congress is necessary for strengthening local authority, especially financial power.[27]

Disclosure of budget information is a sort of government's behavior which depends largely on the government's own moral consciousness. The scale is rather flexible as in some regions the budget information is announced on websites so that the deputies to the People's Congress can have timely supervision, while in other regions even the deputies cannot obtain basic data of government financial revenues and expenditures.

The work of disclosure of budget information must be guaranteed by the legal system. Transparency of government budget must be at first established based on a sound legal system because the more the disclosure of the budget is made compulsory, the more transparent will the budget be. In many countries, transparency of financial budget is effectively implemented through legislation. For example, in the U.S., according to the Freedom of Information Act and Government in the Sunshine Act, the items and the amounts of financial expenditures are required to be opened in order to be supervised by the public society and public opinions. As for China's financial regulations system, the legal system is obviously imperfect and the legislative level is too low.

Although the Regulation on Government Information Openness that was passed at the No. 165 executive meeting of the State Council on January 17, 2007 and came into effect on May 1, 2008 clearly stipulates that the government must open financial budget, final accounts report, the items, bases and standards of administrative fees and the catalogs, and standards and implementation of government procurement, there is no special article and provision on openness and transparency of government budget in the current Budget Law in China. A large portion of the current financial legislation are administrative regulations or departmental rules.

---

[27] Ren Xi-rong. Budget Supervision and Financial Democracy: Growth of the Power of Budget Supervision of the People's Congress. *Journal of University of Political Science of East China*, 2009, (5): 103–104.

Since the levels of the laws are not high enough, effectiveness of implementation will somewhat be affected, thus lowering transparency of the government budget.[28]

In the context of strengthening the goal of openness of budget information, we should pay attention to the complete process of information for budgetary supervision. According to the Regulation for the Implementation of the Budget Law, the comprehensive budget system consists of the government public budget, the state-owned assets operation budget and the social security budget. Yet even after 10 years, the state-owned assets management budget and social security budget have not been established. Although work of budgetary compilation of state-owned capital management has started at the central level, disputes over the power of budgetary compilation and the approval process reflect how much rights (to know and to make decision) the citizens have in supervision over state-owned assets and the revenues.

The frequent incidents of embezzlement and misuse of social security funds actually reflect deficiencies of the democratic system of administrative and investment management of the social security funds.[29] In China, non-budgetary funds of the local governments has almost reached the scale equal to the budgetary funds and it would impose a great challenge on China's governmental governance and social stability if the non-budgetary funds are out of the scope of budgetary supervision. It will undoubtedly be a good opportunity for China to promote constitutionalism if the chance of constitutional construction of the control system of financial revenues and expenditures is grasped. Since the government department holds the power of rational legal violence and is in a position of monopoly, it is difficult for the society to impose constitutional constraints and the Constitution is likely to be violated. Therefore, it needs rational allocation of the financial powers between the departments of authority in order to avoid constitutional violation.

There are constitutional deficiencies in China's financial system and there are no substantive checks and balances and separation of powers

---

[28] Li Yan. Exploration in Analysis of Budget Transparency from the Perspective of Democratic Supervision. *Journal of University of Central Finance*, 2007, (12): 5.

[29] Liu Jian-wen. Constitutionalism and Chinese Financial Democracy. *Tax Research*, 2008, (4): 5–6.

in the political powers. The financial powers are not reasonably allocated in the legislatures, administrative organs, and the judicial organs. More financial powers are held by the administrative organs while the financial powers necessary for the legislatures and judicial organs are insufficient. Abuse of financial powers in China cannot be solved only by general laws. It must start from the Constitution and have public finance constitutionalized with the legal principles of taxation and budget. Furthermore, it is necessary to grasp the constitutional definition of the powers of borrowing in the administrative organs and the principles of checks and balances on the financial powers.[30]

2. Legislation of Budget and Realization of Civil Rights

1. From the perspective of constitutionalism, the process of civic participation in the budgetary supervision process is the requirement of the principle of sovereignty belonging to the people and is specific embodiment of the principle in the field of control of government financial powers. The civil society must take part in the public budget and only in this way can the government truly better allocate the resources to achieve the basic functions of providing public services. From the point of view of financial history, England is the country where the financial restraint system was earliest established, i.e. the people started constitutionalism by struggling to participate in supervision and constraint of the financial powers of the King. Some historians and jurists even shared the point of view that the history of constitutionalism of the human being is essentially a history of financial struggle.

Control of the process of a country's financial revenues and expenditures is equal to control of the foundation of exercise of all authorities in the country. In modern society, supervision of the government by citizens is effected by the representative agencies, but the citizens' direct participation in supervision should not be replaced by supervision by the deputies to the People's Congress. In contrast, currently in China, the civil society's participation in supervision over government behaviors is a

---

[30] Wang Jin-feng. Regulations of Financial Powers from the Constitutional View. *Local Finance Studies*, 2009, (6): 50–51.

powerful supplement for supervision of the People's Congress. The citizen's participation in supervision is a system in response to information openness of public financial revenues and expenditures. The state should continue to build and improve the legal system for the citizens' participation and expand the channels of participation.

Since the public can obtain the right of supervision over government financial revenues and expenditures dominated by the principle of popular sovereignty, a series of financial rights of the civil society will be derived. The exercise of these rights cannot be separated from the citizens' participation in budgetary supervision. Since the taxpayers directly feel the relationship between the budget revenues and expenditures and their present and future interests, they naturally are related with the public budget. Under general circumstances, the less the taxpayers understand the process of public budget, the more freedom the implementers of budget have in their actions; so it is difficult to make a transparent, clear, and effective budget. Increase of supervision of the taxpayers over public budget can drive the government departments to make more efforts to protect the basic rights of the taxpayers and improve the level of performance of public budget so that the taxpayers and the public society become beneficiaries from public budget.[31]

In general, public participation in budgetary supervision is to cooperate with the deputies to the People's Congress to supervise in the People's Congress session or in the process of implementation, compilation, amending, and adjusting of the budget. The civil society gives the People's Congress and the deputies their opinions on public financial revenues and expenditures and establishes a mechanism to allow civil society to effectively urge the People's Congress to supervise the budget through a variety of communication of information. In recent years, all over the country, there has been a lot of practice of grass roots participation in budgetary supervision, however the degree and level of openness is not uniform.

In some regions, the citizen can even attend the meetings on budgetary supervision of the provincial Standing committee of the People's Congress. At the local government level in the U.S., the main mechanism

[31] Sun Kai. On Public Budget Supervision Mechanism. *Financial Research*, 2007, (10): 31.

for citizen participation in the budget includes public hearings, citizen or consumer questionnaire, civic leaders and civic interest group meetings, citizens' advisory council, government official meetings, citizen juries and so on. In the U.S., citizen participation has a long history as civil community appeared earlier than the government. Hearing system and advisory committee are two traditional ways of civic participation in public decision-making. After rise of citizen participation in budget, these traditional patterns have also been used for the same.[32]

The objective of constitutionalism is to establish public-services-oriented responsible governments in the rule of law. Democracy itself is a sort of rule of law based on consultation. As to a budget, the state departmentalism was overemphasized in China in the past rather than interactions between government and the public society. The budget, which is related to the most direct government behavior concerning the daily life of the public, needs consultations between the citizens and the government for the most. By participating in the compilation of the budget, the citizens directly take part in the budgetary process, which include various discussions, allocation of public resource, and supervision over government financial revenues and expenditures, which is an approach to accept constitutional and democratic training and can contribute to coordination of the interests of all segments of the social society in a legal environment. Therefore, the state should gradually remove the obstacles and solve the matter of principle at the level of the Constitution, allowing the provinces to make local regulations on civic participation in budget in detail according to their specific circumstances. Meanwhile, the deputies to the People's Congress need more trainings as they are a bridge of communication between the public and the legislature and after all they hold the right to vote on behalf of the people.

2. The democratic system of budget participation and constitutional fundamental rights. Public financial income is the result of the citizens' delivery of their private property and of course the civil society is the final beneficiary of public finance. Such logic determines that the public is fully

---

[32] Ma Jun, Luo Wan-ping. Civil participation in Budget: Experiences for U.S. Local Government. *Journal of Central China Normal University* (*Humanities and Social Sciences*), 2006, (7): 27.

justified in their paying attention to information of the public budget. The complete system of public budgetary supervision consists of not only legislative and macro-supervision of the People's Congress and daily supervision over government internal matters but also approaches to ensure supervision of the public and news media. Budget process not only affect the distribution of power but also influences decisions in policy and spending. That is, budget process is often an important tool for democratic participation and responsibility.

There is a necessity for local citizens to participate in the budgetary process. The focus of the municipal budget is different from the federal budget. Federal government budget is mainly focused on macro issues such as government planning and deficit. But the municipal government is a direct provider of public services so that the deputies between the political parties, administrative agencies, legislatures, and interest groups that the federal and state government faces are not obviously reflected in the budget of the municipal government. For the municipal government, the main pressure comes from responsibility for the citizens. For example, how the citizens express a variety of demands of interests? How the government hears and adopts these demands? Therefore, in order to solve these problems, tax politics must be followed closely.[33]

Budget, concerning the property relations between the citizens and the government, is presentation of the contradiction between public powers and private rights and also is the most valuable issue in the Constitution. The local government is the government which directly provides public services and needs channels facilitating direct public involvement in financial revenues and expenditures, otherwise it is difficult to talk about budgetary democracy or financial democracy. Unfortunately there are no provisions on citizen participation in budget process on the level of the Budget Law in China. In some provinces such as Guangdong, Zhejiang, and Beijing, the local regulations just generally mention the citizens' rights to participate in budgetary supervision and there are no specific operational articles or even classification of the citizen's participation in the budget.

[33] Niu Mei-li. Citizenship and Public Budget — The Road of Democratic Governance. *Public Administration Review*, 2008, (1): 184.

However, from the perspective of constitutionalism, Chinese citizens have a right to participate in the budget. According to Article 2 of the Constitution, the way in which the civil society exercises the right to participate in budget should be organized by the People's Congress at various levels. At the same time, Article 27 of the Constitution stipulates that all state organs and functionaries must rely on the support of the people, keep in close touch with them, heed their opinions and suggestions, accept their supervision and make efforts to serve people. It gives the citizens the right to participate in the government budget process and express their views that the government has an obligation to listen to.

After the budget reform, although openness of the budget process is still low, in some regions, budgetary process is opened to the citizens with promotion of the local government. The financial and economic committee of the People's Congress of Hebei Province held a hearing on the draft budget for educational funds at the provincial level in November 2004 and held a hearing on the draft budget for agriculture, water conservancy, and forestry departments at the provincial level in November 2005. Not only government officials and leaders from integrated departments but also social individuals, parents of students, experts, scholars, and grassroots workers attended the two budget hearings.

On December 25, 2004, Xiangshui County in Jiangsu held a hearing in financial budget for public opinions on 2005 financial budget arrangements. Representatives of cadres of county and township, the community residents, the farmers, school teachers of primary and middle schools, the deputies to the People's Congress and CPPCC members, nearly 100 in total attended the hearing. This model allows the citizens to a certain extent to affect the budget funding arrangements.

In March 2005 in Xinhe Town of Wenling City in Zhejiang Province, the deliberative discussion system established in 1998 was introduced in the budget. In 2006, the People's Congress in the town further improved the budgetary democratic discussion system and developed a system by combiningit with the deputies to the People's Congress system. In the budgetary democratic discussion, the citizens took part in the examination of the People's Congress on the government budget. Although these attempts of the citizen's participation are somewhat deficient, and the Chinese budget process has been lacking openness for a long time, they are undoubtedly very valuable. These explorations provide great inspiration for reconstruction of the relationship between the state and the citizens in the budget.[34]

Some scholars have proposed that the reform of budgetary participation system should be launched at different levels in the laws. On a legal basis, the citizens' participation in budget is not soundly supported in the law and there are no rules for civic participation in the Budget Law. Civic participation in budget lacks legal protection and there are no specific systematic measures to protect the related rights of the citizens. As almost all of the important aspects of civil rights are closely related with the government budget, it is necessary to ensure that the financial budget is held in the hands of the people.

First, it should improve the budgetary legal system on the basis of the Constitution. In the section on fundamental rights and obligations of the citizens, the term that the citizens of the People's Republic of China are entitled to the right of knowledge of the state government activities can be added so as to protect the citizens' orderly participation in the budget. The Budget Law should clearly stipulate that the citizens are an indispensable subject in the budget, so as to ensure that maximum public opinions are reflected in budget resolution, which in turn reflects the public well-being.

Second, it needs to design effective procedures for civic participation. With considerations of China's conditions, a variety of channels of expanding breadth and depth of the people's participation such as the deputies to the People's Congress voting system, budgetary democratic discussion between the deputies to the People's Congress and the government, and budgetary consultations with representatives of the citizens can be adopted in order to promote civic participation in budget.

Third, it should promote openness of budget information. Finally, it needs a sound examination system of constitutional violation to guarantee the citizens' right to participate.[35] In addition, social professional intermediaries and the news media should play a greater role in civic participation

---

[34] Ma Jun. Politics of the Budget Reform in China: Achievements and Plight. *Journal of Sun Yat-sen University* (*Philosophy and Social Science*), 2007, (3): 71.

[35] Dai Ji-tao. Legal Construction of Civil Participation in Budget: From Specification to System. *Journal of Institute of Guangdong Public Administration*, 2010, (6): 67–68.

in the budget process in order to cut down the costs of civic participation, improve efficiency, and increase openness and credibility of the budget.

The current budget reform was firstly promoted by local governments in Hebei, Guangdong and Tianjin, forming two modes of mainstream budget reform of rules-based system and sunshine finance. In the local budget reform, with full-range involvement in budget management processes by the People's Congress at all levels, following the principles of law, based on the system platform of examination of reports on draft budget and final accounts, a local budgetary supervision system where compilation, implementation, and supervision of the budget is separated and mutually restricted is initially built up. In the People's Congress, a special budgetary supervision agency is established to make regulations on supervision and develop measures of budgetary supervision, which reflects strengthening of the capabilities of the People's Congress in budgetary supervision, namely, rise of the power of purse.

Hebei Province is the cradle of the departmental budget reform in China. In 1999, Hebei provincial People's Congress took the lead in introducing budgetary supervision and adopting the policy of both procedural examination and substantive examination in the People's Congress examination of the budget. In 2004 and 2005, the budget hearing system was introduced in the People's Congress examination of budget and it has been adopted in many regions afterwards. In many regions, powers are exercised to actively strengthen supervision over implementation and adjustment of budget by the local People's Congress. Currently, the participatory budget reforms are also underway in other regions. The standing committee of Hebei provincial People's Congress began to hold budget hearings in 2004 and held two more budget hearings in the 2005 government budget funding for education and 2006 funds for agricultural water conservation. Before the hearings, information was released in newspapers aiming to invite people to participate voluntarily. On the hearings, the financial and budgetary departments presented the reasons for the budgetary arrangements and the civil spokesmen stated their opinions which were recorded in documents by relevant departments as important information for the following primary examination. This approach of budget participation is feasible and should be adopted in all provinces.

However, in some regions, it is still extremely difficult for citizens to get access to government financial information. Wen Hong-xiang, a lawyer and resident of Shenyang City in Liaoning province submitted to such departments as the municipal finance bureau, municipal audit bureau and municipal office of openness of government affairs Applications for Openness of Government Information in Shenyang, requiring all the provincial, district, and county government departments in Shenyang to open financial accounts on expenses of official work, reception, entertainment and travel, and undertaking revenues, and the results of the annual financial audit. But the officer from the office of openness of government affairs held that since there was no precedent and since financial information of the government departments was extremely sensitive, it was extremely difficult to achieve openness and thereby may not be accomplished in action.[36] The troubles in applications for government financial information in accordance with the laws imply the great difficulties the civil society faces in participating in the government budget process.

Section 3. The Principle of Budgetary Supervision

China's Constitution recognized the CCP as the leader in all the social matters and the central and local governments must adhere to this principle. Chinese leaders have reiterated that the model of separation of powers will not be adopted, therefore, the budgetary supervision system of the provincial People's Congress must be combined with the intents of the Party leadership with full consideration of needs of the civil society and finally reach the goal of governing the state by law. The guidelines, principles, policies, and resolutions of the Party must be taken into consideration by the People's Congress and its standing committee while supervising the budget. Besides, at the provincial level, members in the Party committee are always the main leaders in the government, so it is difficult to show disagreements between the Party Committee and the government on major issues. The political reality determines that the budgetary supervision of the provincial People's Congress cares about more focal points of

[36] Citizens in Shenyang Asking the Government to Open Entertainment Fees, Officials Thought it is Extremely Difficult. *People's Daily*, 2008, 11 (17).

the provincial leading group (provincial standing committee) and pays more attention to the wide issues concerning social reform, development, and stability.

1. The Principle of Democratic Supervision

Democracy and rule of law is not only the target of modern political society but also the basic principle for exercise of powers by the People's Congress. Based on supervision in accordance with the law, the first principle of work that the Provincial People's Congress should pay attention to in budgetary supervision is to ensure democratic exercise of the powers. First, the People's Congress should collectively make resolutions, exercise state powers according to the legal procedures and collectively make examination at meetings through a voting system. Article 4 of Law on the Supervision of Standing Committee of People's Congress at Various Levels stipulates that the standing committee of People's Congress at various levels shall, according to the principle of democratic centralism, exercise supervisory powers collectively.

When the People's Congress exercises the powers of making decision and supervision over public finance and manages state affairs on behalf of all the citizens, it must be legitimate and in a careful way. Representative organs have the power to approve budget but it cannot be used arbitrarily and it is constrained in many ways. Firstly, the representative bodies should respect the checks and balances system of the powers in the budget process. For instance, exercise of the right to amend budget should be limited without infringing the right of budgetary compilation of the administrative organs, and the resolution of budget approval shall retain appropriate space for implementation of budget by the executive organs.

Second, budget approval of the representative bodies should be consistent with prior legislation. For instance, social security, debt discharge, and judicative expenses have explicit legal standards. In the Education Law, the Compulsory Education Law, the Agricultural Law, and Science and Technology Progress Law, there are quantitative requirements for financial investment in education, agriculture, science, and technology. Articles 12 and 13 of China's Budget Law stipulate that the higher standing committee of the People's Congress has the power to annul normative documents violating the Constitution, laws or administrative rules and regulations made by the lower standing committee of the People's Congress.

Finally, budget approval of the representative bodies should follow the rules of budget itself such as sound financial doctrine, balance of revenue and expenses, reasonable debt scale, and structure. Based on the principle of annual budget, voting on years of budget is not allowed. Even if the rules are not translated into law, they should become effective constraints of budget approval.[37]

The objective of democratic budgetary supervision of the People's Congress is to protect the fundamental rights of citizens. On the fifth plenary session of the 17th central committee of the CCP, several rights in democratic politics including the right to know, right to participate, right to express, and right to supervise were proposed. These rights are also important in the process of budgetary supervision. Participation in the People's Congress budgetary supervision process mainly refers to participation in the People's Congress examination and approval of financial revenues and expenditures, similar to a hearing system.

The basis of a participation system is financial transparency, which means the protection of the citizens' right to know, right to participate, right to express, and right to supervise in the process of participation in budgetary supervision. It requires abandoning the conventional thought of regarding the budget as confidential. In the past, the deputies to the People's Congress had no chance to even obtain detailed budget statements. The budgetary documents would be taken away after they were reviewed for a short time at the People's Congress session.

The voice of participation in management of state affairs is increasingly higher than ever. Financial revenues and expenditures is one of the most interesting fields of civic participation in supervision. There have been various forms of civic participation in supervision in the grass roots community. The civil society is most qualified to have a strong voice in the allocation of financial resources as a large number funds of ecological and environmental protection, investment in education, social security, medical facilities, and

[37] Yan Hai. Budget Democracy: Construction Based on the Power of Budget Approval. *Chongqing Social Science*, 2007, (4): 105.

housing security closely concern the livelihood of the people. As the scope of vulnerable groups is expanding in the current society, the importance of democratic decision-making deserves more attention in decision-making and management of government public affairs. The People's Congress needs to consider more opinions and interests of the vulnerable groups. Participation in supervision in this way will enable the civil society to truly feel the relationship between public finances and their livelihood.

China's market economy reform demands political development. With the development of market economy and increase of civic wealth, independent personality and civil society are taking shape. Chinese people have become increasingly intense, spontaneous, and conscious in struggles for their rights and protection of the rights. The deputies to the People's Congress in China are organized and elected as planned by the Party. According to a survey, the reason why individual voters take part in the election of the deputies to the People's Congress is that the candidate mainly wants to achieve the target of protecting his economic rights by enhancing the political position.

It should be noted at the same time that the universality of democracy and specialty of public finance are somehow contradictive. Specific requirements need to be satisfied if governments want all the citizens to indirectly participate in the process of budgetary supervision. For instance, information provided in the process of preparation and implementation of the budget should be accurate and not too general. If necessary, the People's Congress should often turn to professional organizations for support in supervision, asking authoritative public institutions for professional advice. In the specific process of supervision, the People's Congress can even integrate social audit institutions with national audit institutions to make up for the deficiency of the national examination power.

2. The Principles of Supervision in Accordance with the Laws

After the human society's transformation from moral governance to constitutional governance, the authority of the Constitution comes from the people or their common will. People are the only legitimate body of power making the constitution, which is a primordial creative power prior to the existence of a state power. Supervision in accordance with the law is the criteria of work and the principle of supervision of the People's Congress. The Law on the Supervision of Standing Committee of People's Congress at Various Levels was adopted at the 23rd meeting of the standing committee of the 10th National People's Congress of the People's Republic of China on August 27, 2006.

The third chapter of the above law is designated for examining and approving final accounts, hearing and deliberating the plans for national economy and social development and the reports on the implementation of budgets and the audit reports as well. Both Articles 15 and 16 set the time when the standing committee of the People's Congress imposes budgetary supervision and when the provincial government submits the reports on plans of budget, implementation and adjustment of budget, which largely solved the issue of information asymmetry in the People's Congress supervision over the government budget.

Article 17 provides that adjustment of budget in implementation should be approved by the People's Congress. The State Council or the local people's government at or above the county level shall submit the adjustment scheme to the standing committee of the People's Congress for examination and approval. It also provides that it is imperative to rigorously control the capital adjustment among different budgetary items. Where the capital arranged for agriculture, education, science and technology, culture, public health and social security, etc. in the budget needs to be adjusted or reduced, the State Council or the local people's government at or above the county level shall report it to the standing committee of the People's Congress for examination.

It also provides that the relevant competent department of the State Council or of the local people's government at or above the county level shall, within one month before the standing committee of the People's Congress, hold a meeting to examine and approve the budget adjustment scheme, submit the preliminary scheme on budget adjustment to the Financial and Economic Committee of the People's Congress for preliminary examination or submit it to the relevant working body of the standing committee for soliciting opinions. In the current context that the budgetary supervision system is not sound, the People's Congress shall focus on budgetary supervision over key points, concentrate on detailed investigations of selected departments or special funds in order to obtain comprehensive information for supervision and actively make special investigations into behaviors of violation, corruption, and malfeasance.

According to the existing budgetary supervision system in China, it has basically formed a relatively complete system consisting of a series of laws, regulations and policies such as Rules of Procedure for the National People's Congress, Regulation for the Implementation of the Budget Law of the People's Republic of China, Decisions on Strengthening Management of Non-budgetary Funds by the State Council, Audit Law of the People's Republic of China, Regulations for the Implementation of the Audit Law of the People's Republic of China, Interim Regulation of Audit of Implementation of Central Budget, and Decisions on Strengthening of Examination and Supervision of Central Budget on the basis of the Constitution, Budget Law, and Supervision Law.

It is the constant reform of the laws that supplies systematic support for establishment of budgetary democracy in China. Based on the budgetary democracy, a new system, in which the Party committee, the government, and the public take part orderly in democratic decision-making and consultation of public affairs, is steadily established and the level and ability of democratic governance of the government is gradually promoted.[38] In the 1980s, the local People's Congress and standing committee in many regions have developed normative documents concerning budgetary supervision and also made specific provisions on budgetary supervision. For instance, the Anhui Province developed Interim Procedures for Budget Management in 1988 and detailed the principles of partial adjustment of the budget, making it operational in practice. In the late 1980s, the People's Congress in Sichuan, Hebei, Chongqing, and other provinces, cities and counties (districts) also made provisions for the budget, marking standardization of exercise of budgetary powers at the local level.[39]

In the existing political and legal system, legal construction of the government budget reform needs to be improved in order for it to support

---

[38] Liu Hui. *Budget Supervision and Democratic Growth: Analysis of the National People's Congress Budget Supervision System from the Political Perspective (1978–2006)*, Shanghai: Fudan University, 2008: 98.

[39] Ren Xi-rong. Budget Supervision and Financial Democracy: Growth of the Power of Budget Supervision of the People's Congress. *Journal of University of Political Science of East China*, 2009, (5): 104.

the budgetary supervision. Deep reform of the fiscal and tax system is needed in establishing a national financial system covering the public financial budget, the state-owned capital management budget, the government budget, and the social security funds budget. It needs to improve transparency of public finance and the mode of audit supervision, and increase independency and authority of the audit and supervision, making it a powerful weapon of the Provincial People's Congress budgetary supervision.

3. The Policy-Oriented Principle

Budget is an embodiment of national policies. As leadership of the Party is the fundamental reality of the country and China's socialist market economy is undergoing rapid growth, the budget process and the policy process cannot be separated although the decisions must be made in accordance with the laws. As various regions differ much in development in China, the terms of making decisions in different provinces must master the direction, focus on the characteristics of local economic and social development, and make decisions in budget according to the state's fiscal and economic policies and social development. Finance should serve and in return promote the national economic and social development.

The laws and regulations such as the Budget Law, the Agricultural Law, the Education Law, the Compulsory Education Law, and the Science and Technology Law put special requirements for the policies and arrangements of budgetary expenditures in important fields such as social security, public health, and housing security. In the process of budgetary implementation and budget adjustment concerning livelihood and public interests of the people, policies of the Party committee should be simultaneously taken into consideration. Budgetary supervision is a complex task of upholding the Party's leadership, with people as the masters and rule of law.

The People's Congress needs to check whether the government budget reflects major financial and economic policies of the country and macro-control goals and priorities of the local Party committee and the government. The general principle of the Provincial People's Congress supervision over all adjustments and changes of budget and structure is to ensure the increase of statutory appropriation in education, agriculture, science and technology, social security, housing security, and public health services and also improve the scale and proportion of general transfer payments and promote social equity and harmonious development.

2010 was the fiscal year of the Shanghai World Expo, and the Shanghai government stressed in the 2010 draft budget that according to the general requirements of the State Council on maintaining continuity and stability of macroeconomic policy and improving pertinence and flexibility of the policies, city-level financial expenditure budget arrangements continue to adhere to the principle of three focal points. The third principle was focus on harmony which obviously reflected the requirements of coordinating with Shanghai World Expo events, including construction of the supervision system of safe production and food and drug safety, strengthening of monitoring and early warning of urban public health emergencies and measures of prevention and control, resolving historical issues and outstanding social conflicts, strengthening and improving social management, prevention and handling emergencies, and promoting social harmony and stability.

Chapter 2

Overview of the System of Budgetary Supervision of Provincial People's Congress

Section 1. Changes of the Budgetary Supervision System of Provincial People's Congress

1. The Background of Changes of the System

Since the tax-sharing reform in 1994 in China, the revenues of the central and local governments have largely increased. But the tax-sharing is actually just the tax division between the central and provincial governments, while there is no specific legal regulation on tax-sharing of the governments below provincial level. Put it in another way, the financial institutional issues below the provincial level have not yet been solved. It means that local governments assume more administrative burdens rather than fiscal revenues. The trend of fiscal centralization at the provincial level is that the proportion of provincial expenditures increased while expenditures at the county and township level declined.

In recent years, Chinese local governments sought funds for development mainly in two ways: borrowing debts and selling lands. Chinese laws stipulate that the local government shall not have financial deficit, that is to say, the local government is not allowed to borrow funds for development. In fact, the debts of local governments are not included in the budgets of the government, so it is extremely difficult to be supervised by the People's Congress. Non-budgetary funds without supervision will reduce the ability of the government to provide fair and effective public services. The existing problem in China is that the local People's Congress and its standing committee lack sound organization and practical supervisory procedures in budgetary supervision. In fact, we need to devote much attention to building of an integral budget under the control of the People's Congress rather than sharing the revenues between all levels of governments.

Based on central superior laws, every province has made local laws and regulations on budgetary supervision, which becomes a legal system of highest effectiveness in guiding the work of budgetary supervision of the local People's Congress. Most of the provinces have also already established the financial and economic committee or budget committee of the People's Congress. Others have at least set up an office of budgetary supervision. In the past, the People's Congress was considered only as a rubber stamp by the civil society as it always passed the public budgets without any disagreement. But in recent years, more and more deputies to the People's Congress have been trying to turn budgetary supervision into substantial supervision from being just a procedural supervision.

2. Formation of the Basic Legal Framework

Although it seems that the reform of the national financial system is not directly related to the development of democratic politics, it literally reflects changes of the underlying constitutionalism. Constraints on the fiscal revenues and expenditures have been changing as the power of purse developed. Several rounds of budget reforms launched by the government are the outcome of the representative agencies' exercise of the power of supervising on behalf of the taxpayers.

With further social and economic development, stronger legal consciousness of civil society, growth of the power of budgetary supervision of the local People's Congress, and innovation of the budgetary supervision system became a typical symbol of development of the Chinese society after the reform and opening up. In particular, after the tax-sharing reform in 1994, local governments had stronger autonomy in budget and impetus for innovation of the budgetary system. Systematic regulations on provincial People's Congress budgetary supervision are getting better and better.

The power of budgetary supervision of the People's Congress at all levels was established shortly after the foundation of the country in 1949.

However, effectiveness of budgetary supervision was limited due to the poor budget management system. From the Common Programme to the Constitution in 1954 and the following amendments, the People's Congress power of budgetary supervision has been confirmed, initially establishing a basis for the institution of budgetary supervision system in China. Article 40 of the Common Programme provided that a budget system shall be instituted to shape the fiscal administration framework between central and local governments. It is the earliest literature of the formal budget management system of the new government.

In 1951, the Interim Regulations on Budget and Final Account issued by the Government Administration Council stipulated the state organizational system of budget, budget powers of the government at various levels, procedures of compilation, examination, approval and implementation of the budgets, and procedures of reporting, approval of final accounts, and establishing the national budgetary system in China. Article 27, Article 49, and Article 58 in the Constitution 195 respectively provided that the National People's Congress has the right to examine and approve the national budget and final accounts; the State Council has the right to implement national economic plan and state budget; the local People's Congress at various levels is entitled to examine and approve the local budget and final accounts.

In 1954, the Local Organization Law stipulated that local People's Congress at various levels is entitled to examine and approve budget and the final accounts, which marked the establishment of this supervision system. The Constitution 1975 and the Constitution 1978 inherited the spirit of financial democracy. The Constitution 1982 further entitled the standing committee of the People's Congress to the power of budgetary supervision and defined the constitutional position of the audit organs in budgetary supervision system for the first time. In addition to the Constitution and the organizational laws, budget administrative regulations, departmental rules and regulations, budget law, audit law, and supervision law were promulgated and implemented, improving the laws and regulations on budgetary supervision.[1]

---

[1] Ren Xi-rong. Budget Supervision and Financial Democracy: Growth of the Power of Budget Supervision of the People's Congress. *Journal of University of Political Science of East China*, 2009, (5): 102.

3. Basis of Systematic Construction

The reform of departmental budget starting in 1999 demanded the government to maintain centralization and unification in finance so as to compile and submit complete, comprehensive, and detailed government budgets for convenient examination. The People's Congress at various levels has enacted decrees and regulations to strengthen the budgetary supervision.

Since the reform of the departmental budget, the number of departmental budgets submitted to the People's Congress for examination gradually increased and budgetary supervision at the local level was steadily strengthened. So far, there are 2408 provincial departmental budgets submitted to the People's Congress for examination and it is more than half of all the departmental budgets. All the departmental budgets are submitted to the People's Congress for examination in Hebei, Guangdong, Liaoning, Heilongjiang, Jiangsu, Anhui, Fujian, Ningxia, Xinjiang, Shenzhen, Xiamen, and Ningbo. Moreover, the submitted budgets are becoming more detailed. Furthermore, most of the provinces have started submitting to the People's Congress integrated budgets including basic expenditures and details of project expenditures. Arrangements of the surplus, central fiscal transfer payments, central special funds, and budget adjustments are included in the documents.[2]

Departmental budget reform provides an opportunity for strengthening budget examination and supervision, and the role of the People's Congress as resource protector in the budget process is enhanced. Three types of specific strategies are adopted: (1) fully playing the role of standing committee of the People's Congress in budget preliminary examination; (2) fully playing the role of the deputies to strengthen budget examination in the People's Congress sessions; and (3) expanding the scope of budget examination and supervision.

As for specific operational content of budgetary supervision, many provinces have created new prospects. Hebei made the first exploration in introducing the provincial budget hearing system. Several provinces provided the provincial People's Congress with the power of budget amendment, Guangdong put forward a real-time online mode of financial

---

[2]Wang Shao-guang, Ma Jun. To 'National Budget' — Financial Transformation and Nation-building. *Public Administration Review*, 2008, (1).

supervision, and Shanghai started the practice of budget management of state-owned funds. The provincial People's Congress and its standing committee of all provinces have established a special finance committee or budget committee as specialized agencies of budget preliminary examination, which further increase the depth and intensity of budgetary supervision and increasingly request provincial governments and government departments to submit more and more detailed departmental draft budgets and steadily intensify inquiry of budget and questioning.

The Ministry of Finance issued the Guiding Opinions of the Ministry of Finance on Further Pushing Forward Information Disclosure of Financial Budget based on The Decree of Government Information Openness in September 2008, stipulating in detail the main contents and methods of information disclosure of financial budget and requiring central government departments and local financial departments at all levels to make active efforts in information disclosure. Furthermore, the document claims to push forward information disclosure on government budgets, departmental budgets, budgetary implementation, fiscal transfer payments, and so on. The financial departments at various levels should frequently open routine affairs, gradually open temporary affairs and open on time affairs concerning vital interests of the public through most popular public media such as the governments' official websites, newspaper, radio, television, and press conferences in accordance with prescribed procedures according to the requirements of government information disclosure relying on the Golden Finance Project, thus establishing a perfect information disclosure system of financial budget step by step.

The purpose of the Guiding Opinions is to protect citizens' right to know about, right to participate in, right to express opinions regarding, and right to supervise the financial budgets and to also ensure that enough financial information is obtained for these purposes. The Ministry of Finance in January 2010 issued a draft for suggestions Notice on Further Promoting Information Disclosure of Local Financial Budget. It stipulates the contents, methods, and scope of information disclosure and requires financial departments at various levels to submit and actively disclose the reports on financial budget, final accounts, and departmental budget in standardized formats. These actions show that the Chinese government becomes aware of the importance of greatly promoting financial information disclosure, and the Chinese social environment is moving towards a good trend of being more mature and open.[3]

Section 2. Origins of the Budgetary Supervision System of Provincial People's Congress

1. The Constitution and Laws

The Constitution. According to Article 2 of The Constitution, all powers in the People's Republic of China belong to the people. The National People's Congress and the local People's Congress at various levels are the organs through which the people exercise state power. The people administer state affairs and manage economic, cultural, and social affairs through various channels and in various ways in accordance with the law. This determines that the provincial People's Congress is the supreme organ of exercising state power on behalf of the people in the province, and the people are involved in management of national and social affairs through the provincial People's Congress in accordance with national laws, exercising the power of supervision.

Supervision over public budget is surely one of the most important aspects of the people's management of national affairs. Article 99 of the Constitution stipulates that the provincial People's Congress has powers to examine and approve economic and social development plans, budget, and the reports on implementation in their respective administrative areas. Article 104 provides that the provincial People's Congress and its standing committee decide all aspects of major issues in their respective administrative areas. This provision also surely includes provincial People's Congress supervision over government budget. Article 110 provides that provincial people's government is responsible for the People's Congress. This provision grants the standing committee of the provincial People's Congress the power of supervision over government budget during the recess of the People's Congress meeting.

[3] Li Yan. Financial Information Disclosure Transparency is the Basis for Budget Supervision and Management. *Financial Research*, 2010, (6): 14, in which original text of Professor Li Yan written in 2009 and the notice was issued in 2010.

As for the authority of budgetary supervision of the local People's Congress in the Constitution, the final expression in the fourth version of the Constitution is that the local People's Congress at and above the county level shall examine and approve the plans for economic and social development, budgets of their respective administrative areas, and the reports on their implementation. According to Article 13, the local People's Congress at or above the county level shall examine the draft general budget and the report on the implementation of the general budget, approve the budget and the report on its implementation. According to Article 39 of Chapter V Examination and Approval of Budgets, the budgets of the local governments at various levels shall be examined and approved by the People's Congress.

Other laws and regulations. Article 9 of the Law of the Deputies to the National People's Congress and the local People's Congress at Various Levels provides that the deputies have the right, in accordance with procedures prescribed by law, to submit to the People's Congress bills and proposals within the scope of its functions and powers. Since approval of the draft budget is one of the functions of the People's Congress, the deputies are entitled to submit the proposals of various views of the draft budget. Many countries have explicit provisions that the legislature and its members have the right to make proposals of amendment to the draft budget and modify an item of the governmental or departmental draft budget.[4]

Article 8 of the Organic Law of the Local People's Congress and Local People's Governments provides that the provincial People's Congress in the administrative area ensures to comply with and implement the Constitution, laws, administrative regulations, and resolutions of the higher People's Congress and implementation of budget and examine and approve economic and social development plans, budgets, and reports on the implementation. Article 44 provides that based on proposals of the people's government, the corresponding level standing committee of the provincial People's Congress decides to adjust part of the economic and social development plans and budgets in the respective administrative areas.

---

[4] China Development Research Foundation. *Public Budgets Reading*, Beijing: China Development Press, 2008: 111.

Article 13 of the Budget Law provides that the local People's Congress at or above the county level shall examine and approve the draft general budget and the report on the implementation, alter or annul inappropriate resolutions made by the standing committee of the People's Congress or the government on budget or final accounts. Article 15 provides that the provincial government compiles the budget of the government, makes report on the draft general budget to the People's Congress, work out the adjustment plan for the budget and submit report to the People's Congress or its standing committee on the implementation of the general budget.

Article 37 provides that the financial department under the State Council shall, one month before the annual session of the National People's Congress, submit the main contents of the draft central budget to the Financial and Economic Committee of the National People's Congress for preliminary examination. Article 54 provides that provincial government budget adjustment plan must be submitted to the standing committee of the People's Congress for examination and approval. Article 55 provides that in case budget adjustments are not approved, the government shall not make any decisions making total expenditures exceed total revenues in the original approved budgets or making an increase of the debt. In case a decision is made in violation of the provisions of the preceding paragraph, the people's congress or the standing committee of the people's congress or the government of higher level shall order a change or annulment of the decision.

Article 56 provides that the provincial governments shall, in receipt of returned funds or subsidies, report the relevant situations to the standing committee of the People's Congress. Article 66 provides that provincial People's Congress and its standing committee exercise supervision over the budget and final accounts of the governments. Article 67 provides that provincial People's Congress and its standing committee have the power to conduct investigations of major issues or specific questions concerning the budget or final accounts; governments, departments, units, or individuals concerned should report the situations and provide the necessary materials in a true manner.

Article 68 provides that when the provincial People's Congress and the standing committee are in session, deputies to the People's Congress or members of the standing committee may, in accordance with the procedures prescribed by law, raise questions or address inquiries concerning the budgets or final accounts to the relevant governments or financial departments, which must promptly answer the questions or inquiries. Article 69 provides that a provincial government, at least twice within each budgetary year, make reports on the budgetary implementation to the People's Congress or its standing committee.

The Law on the Supervision of Standing Committee of People's Congress at Various Levels comprehensively defines budgetary supervision of the standing committee of the provincial People's Congress. The third chapter provides that the standing committee of the People's Congress listens to and examines the reports on economic and social development plan and implementation of the budgets. Article 16 provides that the local people's government at or above the county level shall, during the period from June to September each year, report the conditions on implementing the plan for national economy and social development and the budget to the standing committee of the people's congress.

Article 17 provides that when the plan for national economy and social development or the budget needs to be partially adjusted after it is approved by the people's congress, the provincial people's government should submit the adjustment scheme to the standing committee of the people's congress for examination and approval. It is imperative to rigorously control the adjustment among different budgetary items. When the funds arranged for agriculture, education, science and technology, culture, public health, and social security in the budget needs to be adjusted or reduced, the provincial people's government should report it to the standing committee of the people's congress for examination and approval.

The provincial people's government should, within one month before the standing committee of the People's Congress hold a meeting to examine and approve the budget adjustment scheme, submit the preliminary scheme on budgetary adjustment to the financial and economic committee of the People's Congress for preliminary examination or submit it to the relevant agencies of the standing committee for soliciting opinions. Article 18 lists in detail that the standing committee shall carry out key examination of the report of budgetary implementation, the balance of national debts and the arrangement and use of financial assistance funds granted by the higher levels. Article 20 provides that the members of the standing committee shall submit the opinions about the report on the implementation of the plan for national economy and social development, the report on the budgetary implementation as well as the audit report to the people's government. The people's government should make a written report to the standing committee afterwards. The standing committee can make a resolution on the audit report when necessary. The reports on implementing the plan for national economy and social development, the budget, audit, and opinions shall be circulated to the deputies of the people's congress and be announced to the general public.

Furthermore, Chapter VI of the Supervision Law defines the powers of Inquiry and Interrogatory of the standing committee of the People's Congress and Chapter VII defines the power of investigation of special issues, which are both associated with exercise of the power of budgetary supervision of the People's Congress. As the current Budget Law was enacted in 1994 while the Supervision Law is newly adopted, many points were out of date or not specific. So Chapter III of the Supervision Law is essentially a major supplement of the Budget Law.[5] And then the provinces passed rules of the implementation of the Supervision Law.

Article IV of the Audit Law provides that the provincial people's government should annually present to the standing committee of the People's Congress the audit reports prepared by the audit department on budgetary implementation and other budgetary revenues and expenditures. The standing committee of the People's Congress can make resolutions in audit report, if necessary.

2. Administrative Laws and Regulations

After promulgation of the Budget Law, according to Article 78 of the Budget Law, the State Council issued Regulation for the Implementation of the Budget Law at the end of 1995. The main objective of the regulation is to explain the contents of the Budget Law, and the provisions of explanation have become an important basis for budgetary supervision of the provincial People's Congress. According to paragraph 2 of Article 11 local budgetary revenues in Budget Law refers to the revenues that are brought

[5] Xu Shu-na. Analysis of the Environments of the Local People's Congress Budget Supervision System. *Journal of Shanghai University of Finance and Economics*, 2008, (6): 55.

into the local budgets and that are not shared by the central government according to the system of tax division between the central and local governments, including revenues at the local levels and revenues refunded or subsidized to the local governments by the central government. This provision provides the budgetary supervision range of the provincial People's Congress as many provinces do not have revenues refunded or subsidized by the central government included in provincial budget management.

Article 60 provides that the schemes of budget adjustment shall be made by the government departments of public finance. The schemes on budget adjustment should include the reasons, items, amount, and measures of the adjustment, and the relevant explanations, and those schemes should be, after being examined by the governments, submitted to the standing committee of the People's Congress for examination and approval. Regulation for the Implementation of the Budget Law explains the meaning of the main points for the provincial People's Congress budgetary supervision more in detail and provides more authoritative standards for budgetary supervision of the People's Congress.

Since reform and opening up, non-budgetary funds are growing fast and lack financial management and supervision of the People's Congress. These problems not only cause dispersion of state funds and disorder of public distribution but also increase fixed asset investment and consumptive funds, contributing to the occurrence of irregularities and corruption. Struggling against this situation, in 1996, the State Council issued the No. 29 Document — the State Council Decisions on Strengthening Management of Non-budgetary Funds. Decisions provide that budgetary funds cannot be turned into non-budgetary funds; departmental non-budgetary funds should be included in the financial budget for management. A total of 83 items of administrative charges and fees prescribed by the Ministry of Finance were included in the financial budget. The decision also provides that the people's government at all levels should be supervised by the People's Congress at the responding level over use of non-budgetary funds. The provincial government enjoys much financial freedom in administrative fees and funds, which imposes great challenges in the management of non-budgetary funds, and the provincial People's Congress supervision over non-budgetary funds is extremely important and is a crucial point of anti-corruption.

In 2007, the State Council passed Regulations on Open Government Information with No. 492 Decree. Article 10 emphasizes the scope of disclosure of government information. Promulgation of the regulation to some extent strengthens the legal basis for disclosure of government fiscal information and will urge the government to disclose more complete information as required by the People's Congress for budgetary supervision. The State Council has promulgated a series of regulations and normative documents in financial supervision, such as Decisions on Balance of Revenues and Expenditures and Strict Financial Management and Provisions on Work of Financial Supervision, improving the main system of financial supervision in China.

3. Local Laws and Regulations

Regulations on budgetary supervision. Provinces have passed local laws and regulations on budgetary supervision. These regulations are relatively practical and suitable for actual requirements of local economic and social development and substantially guide budgetary supervision of provincial People's Congress and are beneficial supplements to national laws and regulations on budgetary supervision. By the end of 2006, the People's Congress in all provinces, autonomous regions, and municipalities have made regulations, provisions, or decisions for strengthening examination and supervision of budgets (see table in the following pages). These local laws and regulations have made improvement and innovation in the examination of the draft budget, special audit, inquiry, investigations into major issues, budget adjustment, examination of final accounts, supervision of use of surplus revenue and non-budgetary funds, preparation of consolidated budget, and legal liability. Some typical experiences of budgetary supervision in practice were created: Jiangxi Province promotes procedural and substantive examination and supervision; Shanghai focuses on training representatives and earlier examination; Guangdong pays attention to detailed budgetary compilation and sharing of financial information; Shenzhen deepens the individual audit and audit of performance; Henan deputies inquire into joint signature.[6]

---

[6]Zhao Wen. *Concise Reading of Budget Examination and Supervision of Local People's Congress*, Shanghai: Fudan University Press, 2008: 154–159.

Legislation of Budgetary Supervision by the Provincial People's Congress

	Provinces	Title of Regulations	Time of Approval
1	Beijing	Regulation for budgetary supervision	December, 1996
2	Heilongjiang	Regulation for budgetary supervision	December, 1998
3	Liaoning	Regulations on budgetary examination and supervision	July, 1999
4	Shanxi	Regulation for budgetary supervision	November, 1999
5	Guangxi	Regulation for budgetary supervision	March, 2000
6	Shaanxi	Decisions of strengthening examination and supervision of provincial budgets	March, 2000
7	Zhenjiang	Decisions of examination and supervision of budget	August, 2000
8	Ningxia	Decisions of budgetary supervision	August, 2000
9	Neimenggu	Measures of examination and supervision of budget	October, 2000
10	Jiangsu	Decisions of examination and supervision of budget	December, 2000
11	Yunnan	Regulations on budgetary examination and supervision	December, 2000
12	Shandong	Regulations on budgetary examination and supervision	December, 2000
13	Jilin	Regulations on budgetary examination and supervision	January, 2001
14	Hubei	Decisions of examination and supervision of budget	January, 2001
15	Guangdong	Regulations on approval and supervision of budget	February, 2001
16	Hainan	Regulation for budget examination and supervision	February, 2001

(*Continued*)

(Continued)

	Provinces	Title of Regulations	Time of Approval
17	Jiangxi	Decisions of examination and supervision of budget	April, 2001
18	Qinghai	Regulations on the budget review	July, 2001
19	Shanghai	Regulations on budget examination and supervision	August, 2001
20	Hunan	Regulations on budget examination and supervision	September, 2001
21	Hebei	Regulations on budgetary supervision	September, 2001
22	Tianjin	Regulations on budget examination and supervision	October, 2001
23	Anhui	Regulations on budget examination and supervision	January, 2002
24	Henan	Regulations on budgetary supervision	January, 2002
25	Gansu	Regulations on budget examination and supervision	February, 2002
26	Fujian	Decision of strengthening work of examination and supervision of budget	May, 2002
27	Sichuan	Decision of strengthening work of examination and supervision of provincial budget	May, 2002
28	Guizhou	Regulations on budget examination and supervision	May, 2002
29	Tibet	Decision of strengthening work of examination and supervision of budget at automous regional level	September, 2002
30	Chongqing	Regulations on budgetary supervision	May, 2004

Note: Enforcement Measures for Budget Management of Xinjiang Production and Construction Corps was reviewed and passed on January 7, 2000 at the first meeting of the commanders of the Corps.

New Rules of Budgetary Supervision of the Provincial People's Congress

	New Rules	Number of Provinces
1	Feedback of the main methods and suggestions of preliminary examination	14
2	To conduct a special audit	25
3	To inquire and challenge	13
4	To make investigations into major or specific issues	10
5	To hold hearings on major issues	4
6	To strengthen examination and supervision of budget adjustments	20
7	To propose budget amendment	3
8	To strengthen examination and supervision of the use of surplus revenue	16
9	To report draft final accounts once again	1
10	To strengthen supervision on the use of non-budgetary funds	16
11	To prepare consolidated budget	4
12	To prepare interim budget	1
13	To report and prosecute violations	5
14	To investigate the legal liabilities of violations	17

While considering legislative authority, exploration of budgetary democracy in which budgetary supervision of the People's Congress is the core can be conducted starting from construction of provincial institutions. Compared with the central government, the provincial government has many advantages in meeting the local requirements and consequently can provide better public goods and services, which have great impacts on the local economic environments.[7] The portion of local financial expenditures kept growing in the periods of financial responsibility and tax-sharing

[7]Lin Yi-fu, Liu Zhi-qiang. China's Financial Decentralization and Economic Growth. *Journal of Peking University* (*Philosophy and Social Science*), 2000, (4): 6, 13.

reform, from 45% in 1981 to up to 72.3% in 2004, which implied that local governments had more and more financial control powers.

Besides, the variables of financial acts of the local government have great influences on efficiency of expenditures. For instance, budgetary revenues have positive influences on efficiency of expenditures while non-budgetary revenues are negatively related with efficiency of expenditures.[8] Data provided in the World Development Report of Government in the Changing World in 1997 shows that in developed countries, the provincial government's fiscal expenditures are about 30% on average of total expenditures of governments and 60% even in the most decentralized countries such as Canada and Japan. In the 1990s, the average percentage of developing countries was 14%, transitional economies 26%, and the United States less than 50%. In China, provincial fiscal expenditures keep nearly 70% of the total national fiscal expenditures since over a decade.[9]

All People's Congress of all provinces have legislative and the institutions that are relatively perfect and practical in implementation have positive impacts on economic and social development, thus creating a competitive situation between the provinces to a certain extent. Compared with the central government budget, compilation and implementation of provincial budgets are much more complicated so that studies of provincial budgetary supervision are of greater importance.

Since the 1980s, People's Congress of many provinces began to emphasize more specific work for budgetary supervision. Anhui, Sichuan, Hebei, and Guangdong began to make detailed normative documents on budgetary supervision, marking the beginning of the era of exercise of the powers of provincial budgetary supervision in a standard and democratic way. Since the 1990s, with introduction of tax-sharing and dual budgetary system to strengthen management of non-budgetary funds and increase of authority over the administrative affairs, the local People's Congress made

---

[8] Chen Shi-yi, Zhang Jun. Did Financial Decentralization Improve efficiency of the Expenditures of Chinese Local Government? — Evidence from Provincial Governments from 1978 to 2004. *Competition for Growth — Politics and Economics of the Growth in China*, Shanghai: Shanghai People's Publishing House, 2008: 228–229, 249.

[9] Zhang Jun. *The Reform Unknown to the Public*, Beijing: CITIC Publishing House, 2010: 140–141.

a large number of local laws and regulations on standardization of the power of budgetary supervision.

Since the beginning of this century, budget reforms based on department budget have gradually started, making compilation and implementation of budget more scientific and standardized and the laws and regulations of the People's Congress on budgetary supervision further improved. The People's Congress of all provinces has made local laws and regulations on budgetary examination and supervision under the guidance of the Constitution and the Budget Law, the National People's Congress and Local People's Congress Law, and the Law of Supervision of the People's Congress at All Levels, carrying out practices and explorations in budget reform. More importantly, these local laws and regulations have made improvement and innovation in preliminary examination of draft budget, special audit, challenge and enquiry, investigation of major issues, budget adjustments, final accounts examination, supervision of surplus revenue, supervision of non-budgetary funds, preparation of the consolidated budget, and legal responsibilities.[10] Some provinces have made a breakthrough in draft budget amendment system.

The Budget Law in China generally does not provide the People's Congress and the deputies the right to amend the draft budget. Yet in recent years, the deputies to the People's Congress in some provinces are permitted to amend budgets through local laws such as decrees, decisions or regulations on budgetary supervision. The Hubei Province passed Enforcement Measures of The Budget Law in July 1996, in which the provisions of Article 16 stipulate that the special committee of the People's Congress and deputies to the People's Congress can propose amendment to the meeting of the People's Congress. When amendments to the draft budget are agreed to be submitted by the meeting of presidium and passed by the People's Congress, the government should amend the draft budget in accordance with the resolution.

The Shanxi Province passed Regulations on Budgetary Supervision in Shanxi Province in November 1999, in which Article 11 stipulates that the financial and economic committee of the People's Congress can propose

---

[10] Zhu Jin. Local People's Congress Budget Supervision: Status, Problems and Solutions. *Yangtze River Forum*, 2008, (6): 55.

amendment of the budget to meeting of presidium, but there is no following procedural regulation. The Yunnan Province passed Regulations on Budgetary Examination and Supervision in Yunnan Province in December 2000, in which Article 12 stipulates how to vote the draft budget with amendment. The Hainan Province passed Regulations on Budgetary Examination and Supervision in Hainan Province in February 2001, in which Article 15 stipulates in detail the number of representatives to propose amendments to the draft budget and the way of voting and Article 16 stipulates subsequent approaches after voting.

Guangdong Province passed Regulations on Budgetary Examination, Approval and Supervision in Guangdong Province in February 2001, in which Article 14 provides the number of representatives to propose amendments to the draft budget and requirements of the proposed amendment of increasing expenditures. The regulations on ways of voting are more detailed and operational. Hebei Province passed Regulations on Budgetary Examination and Supervision in Hebei Province in September 2001, in which Article 15 provides treatment of budget amendment and Article 27 provides the requirements to propose the amendment and the way of voting.

The provincial People's Congress in China has some common characteristics in innovation of the system of power of amendment to the draft budget. In most provinces, the terms are too simple and lack substantive and procedural contents. Some terms just refer to amendment without detailed regulations of proposing the amendment.[11] In the trend of more division of administrative affairs and financial affairs between local and central governments, especially amendment of Budget Law permitting local governments to raise debts, it is well worth to look into the procedures and rules issues in budgetary supervision. In practice, however, the budgetary supervision system in China seems indefensible here and there. The drafters of the Budget Law never expect the budget to be rejected as it is unprecedented. The Constitution, however, grants the People's Congress the veto power.[12]

[11] Ma Jun, Lin Mu-hua. Budget Amendment Powers of the Modern Parliament. *Calls for the Public Budget*, Beijing: Central Compilation and Translation Press, 2008: 103.

[12] Wang Shi-tao. Revision of the Budget Law and Improvement of the Legal System of Budget Supervision. *Financial Studies*, 2005, (3): 91–93.

Other regulations. After the promulgation of the Law of Supervision of the Standing Committee of the People's Congress, the provinces have passed one after another measures for implementing Law of Supervision to regulate in detail the specific contents and methods of budgetary supervision by the provincial People's Congress, usually emphasizing the contents of supervision of the standing committee of the People's Congress, opinions of the deputies, and approaches of information disclosure by the standing committee. The provinces generally make regulations of audit and supervision over implementation of local budgets and make unified regulations on content, time, report and ways of reporting of audit of budgetary implementation.

Apart from Regulations on Examination, Approval and Supervision of Budget in Guangdong (2001), Guangdong also made Measures of Management of Non-budgetary funds, regulating management of non-budgetary funds at the provincial level regarding management of revenues, expenditures, plans of revenues and expenditures, final accounts, supervision, inspection and legal responsibility. Regulations on Audit of Budgetary Implementation in Guangdong (2009) regulates audit and supervision in the process of budgetary implementation.

Article 17 stipulates that the people's government shall, during the period from June to September each year, report to the standing committee of the People's Congress on audit of budgetary implementation and other financial revenues and expenditures of the last year. The audit report should focus on reporting on audit of budgetary implementation. While examining and approving the final accounts, the standing committee of the People's Congress should also examine and approve audit report and make resolution for the report, if necessary.

Article 18 provides that upon receipt of audit opinions, the people's government should promptly respond and report related measures and treatment to the standing committee of the People's Congress within six months. In order to strengthen expenditure management and reform, and establish a scientific, standardized, and efficient allocation and management system of financial resources, Guangdong Province also made Experiment Scheme of Performance Assessment of Financial Expenditures in Guangdong in 2004, providing that if necessary, a special committee of the People's Congress, the deputies and CPPCC members should be invited to attend the evaluation meeting.

The Hubei Province passed Enforcement Measures of the Budget Law, in which Article 34 of Chapter 4 stipulates that the people's government should report to the People's Congress or its standing committee on budgetary implementation at least twice each fiscal year. The standing committee of the People's Congress can organize members and representatives to inspect budgetary implementation, if necessary. As for the major issues in budgetary implementation, representatives can be organized to make investigations. The people's government and relevant departments, units and individuals should accurately report the situation and provide necessary materials. If the standing committee of the People's Congress believes that it is necessary to audit certain matters, the people's government can instruct the audit department to conduct a special audit.

In 2000, Hubei passed Regulations on Supervision of the Standing Committee of the People's Congress. Article 18 provides that the standing committee of the People's Congress conducts supervision over implementation of economic and social development plans, budgets and revenues and expenditures of non-budgetary funds, examines and approves partial adjustment of the budgets and the final accounts. Articles 19, 20, 21, 22, and 23 specifically stipulate the responsibilities of the government and procedures of the standing committee of the provincial People's Congress regarding specific budgetary supervision.

The Shaanxi Province passed Regulations on Budgetary Management in 1990. Articles 16, 17, 18, 19, and 20 of Chapter 3 specifically provide the arrangements of preliminary and key examination of draft budget of the standing committee of the People's Congress. Chapter 4 further stipulates the supervision procedures on partial budget adjustment and major issues investigation. Regulations on Audit and Supervision of Budgetary implementation and Other Financial Revenues and Expenditures in Shaanxi Province passed in 2001 regulates the contents and ways of audit and supervision of budgetary implementation, in which Article 15 stipulates that the people's governments should submit annually to the standing committee of the People's Congress audit reports of the budgetary implementation and other financial revenues and expenditures.

According to the practice of disclosure of budget information in various provinces, the work of disclosure greatly differs and lacks a unified standard. Since disclosure of budget information is significantly related to protection of fundamental rights of the citizens, especially the right to know, a unified standard must be set up. Otherwise, it would become eventually difficult for the work of disclosure of budget information in the provinces to satisfy the strong desire of the civil society for supervision over the financial revenues and expenditures of the government.

There are no specific laws and regulations on openness of government information since 1949. The Budget Law made in the 1990s failed to make special regulations on disclosure of budgetary information. Regulations on Openness of Government Information by the State Council in 2007 stipulates financial budgets and final accounts report as key information to be opened, which is regarded as the first law regarding disclosure of budgetary information. According to the practice of regulations on disclosure of budgetary information in various provinces, they all make regulations on disclosure of information at provincial level for implementing Regulations on Openness of Government Information and most of them do not make specific regulations on disclosure of budgetary information except Jiangxi and Shanghai. Shanghai has made Measures for Further Promoting Implementation of Municipal Disclosure of Budgetary Information, definitely mentioning to promptly disclose revenues and expenditures monthly or quarterly.

Some municipal departments which are closely related with the interests of the public will make experiments in initiative disclosure of the total number of public budgetary expenditures and project expenditures. What the public are most concerned about are funds in support of reconstruction of Dujiangyan city after the earthquake, the bus industry subsidies to public traffic and aids to the students from poor families, other special funds of transfer fees of state-owned land-use right, toll of the roads constructed by loans, new motor vehicle quota auction, and other financial funds such as welfare lottery and sports lottery, which will also be regularly disclosed to the public community after the implementation of the program.

The Jiangxi Province issued Opinions for Further Promotion of the Work of Disclosure of Administrative Affairs of the Financial Departments in April 2006. Opinions require that the financial departments at all levels should disclose what the people most concerned about want for the sake of right to know, so as to serve the public and be supervised by the people. According to the provisions of the Opinions, it is a relatively comprehensive set of rules and regulations on provincial disclosure of budgetary information. Opinions firstly provide four principles: Disclose in accordance with the laws, comprehensive and true, focus on actual effects and convenient for supervision. The key contents, approaches, and procedures of disclosure to be disclosed are specifically listed. Such a relatively comprehensive regulation on provincial disclosure of budgetary information is indeed rare in China.

4. Departmental Rules and Regulations

In recent years, the Ministry of Finance has promulgated in succession Specific Rules for Financial Examination and Inquisition, Measures for Work of Financial Examination, Regulations on Financial Supervision, Regulations on Management of the Funds Allocated by Central Budget, Interim Provisions on Regulating Discipline of Financial Management, Guiding Opinions for Report to the People's Congress on Financial Draft Budgets and Final Accounts and Their Implementation, accelerating the pace of Financial Legislation and basically forming the legal framework of budgetary supervision.

In 2005, the Ministry of Finance, in the form of a notice, issued to various provinces the Guiding Opinions for Report to the People's Congress on Financial Draft Budgets and Final Accounts and Their Implementation. The purpose of making the Opinions is to regulate the contents and format of the local governments to the local People's Congress on draft budget, final accounts, and their implementation so as to facilitate the People's Congress to examine and approve the reports. Opinions regulate the types and requirements of the reports, delivery time of the reports, basic contents of the draft budget, and how the government should report to the standing committee of the People's Congress on main contents, specific items and the main reasons for increase or deduction in case of budgetary adjustments in implementation.

In 2006, a supplementary notice of the Opinions was issued. It stipulates that the tax return and subsidies for the local governments should be fully included in the budget of the government. Meanwhile, the budget should reflect tax returns and subsidies for the subordinates. Notice on Compilation of 2007 Central and Local Budgets once again clearly required the provincial governments, autonomous regions, and municipalities to have incomes of central tax return and subsidies fully included in the total provincial budget so as to be supervised by the People's Congress.

Section 3. Main Contents and Procedures of Budgetary Supervision of Provincial People's Congress

1. Supervision in the Process of Coordination of Making Budget

In general, the provincial governments will make explanations of policies for budgetary revenues and expenditures of the next year in the notice of making draft budget of this year following the relevant requirements of the State Council. They will also submit the intention and policy recommendations of the government budget to the provincial People's Congress, and the special committee of the People's Congress will often attend the meetings of the government financial departments before making budgets and take part in discussions of preparation for budget of the next year after fully absorbing opinions of professionals in the civil society towards the budget.

At this stage the budget committee of the provincial People's Congress will send the deputies to various government departments to review budget reports, mainly analyzing implementation of the budget, collecting civil expectations for the budget, reviewing and making suggestions for the reports of relevant departments on implementation of the budget, and exchanging ideas for making the draft budget before the budget report and the draft budget is handled in a legal procedure. They will eventually propose a budget analysis report. In the supervision of different stages of making, amending, implementing, and adjusting the budget, the provincial People's Congress can control the all-round scale and direction of public financial revenues and expenditures in accordance with the standard requirements of these files and truly ensure that the government arrange the revenues and expenditures in accordance with the idea of serving the people, and thus the special committee of the provincial People's Congress can make coordination and communication for the draft budget according to the basic budgeting ideas in advance.

In the Notice of Making Provincial and Local Budgets of the People's Government for 2006, the Gansu Province specified 5 arrangements and points of policies for financial revenues and 9 for financial expenditures. In the arrangement of expenditures, it especially points out that according to the economic and social development, the requirements of deepening the reforms, and the prudent fiscal policies, the central government continues to cut down central budget deficit and national debts and increase regular investment, adjust projects of financial debts and direction and structure of investment of central budget.

Notice of Making Municipal and Regional Budgets for 2007 pointed out that Tianjin should actively adjust and optimize the structure of financial expenditures and put more money in public service sectors; increase expenditures in social affairs, science and technology, and construction of new socialist countryside; solve the issues related to direct and practical interests of the people; promote economic and social development and accelerate building of a harmonious Tianjin; constantly improve the public finance system; promote the equalization of basic public services; and strive to improve the normative, safe, and effective use of financial funds.

Jiangsu Province made Measures of Management of Budgetary compilation of Provincial Departments in 2005, in general pointing out that it should effectively implement sound fiscal policy, continue to implement the guidelines of a balanced budget, having an overall consideration, and keeping expenditures within the limits of revenues; in accordance with the requirements of the building framework of public finance, vigorously adjust the structure of expenditures, optimize allocation of resources, concentrate financial resources on significant, practical, difficult, and urgent issues; further improve the measures of departmental budgetary compilation, detail budgetary compilation and improve budgetary rationality and transparency.

2. Supervision in Daily Implementation of Budget

The Constitution, the Budget Law and the Supervision Law provide the People's Congress with the power of supervision over the budget. But in order to achieve an efficient government, in the process of supervision in practice, the People's Congress supervising all the time every penny of the expenditures of the government is neither realistic nor practical. Therefore, supervision over budgetary implementation is a kind of supervision afterwards, mainly based on the audit results. Audit and supervision are part of budgetary supervision of the People's Congress which has the power to review the audit reports. Article 13 of the Budget Law grants the standing committee of the provincial People's Congress the power of supervision over implementation of budget and all the local laws and regulations on supervision over the provincial budget will list the contents of budgetary implementation to be supervised by the standing committee of the provincial People's Congress.

Article 18 of the Supervision Law lists the key elements of the implementation of budgets to be examined by the standing committee of the provincial People's Congress, which are as follows: (1) Conditions on the balance of the budget; (2) The arrangement of key expenditures and the availability of the funds; (3) The arrangement and use of the incomes in excess of the budget; (4) The establishment and implementation of the budgetary system of the department; (5) Transferring the payment to the public finance at the lower levels; and (6) Conditions on implementing the resolution of the People's Congress on approving the budget. The Supervision Law further provides that after reviewing the audit report, the standing committee of the People's Congress can also deliver a resolution to the government and the government must report implementation of the resolution to the standing committee of the People's Congress.

3. Supervision over Budget Adjustment

Due to social, economic, political as well as other changes in nature, budgetary adjustment in the process of implementation can take place. However, if the People's Congress fails to supervise budgetary adjustment, its authorities of supervision would be doubted and make earlier approval of the draft budgets meaningless, and even breed corruption. Therefore, in addition to supervision over the governments' implementation of the budgets by audit results, the People's Congress should also pay more attention to supervise budget adjustments in the process of implementation, examine rationality of the budget adjustments so as to ensure authority and effectiveness of budgetary supervision.

Article 54 of the Budget Law stipulates that the government shall, regarding indispensable adjustments, work out plans for budget adjustments. The budget adjustment plans of the local governments must be submitted to the standing committee of the People's Congress for examination and approval. Article 55 provides that in case budget adjustments are not approved, the government shall not make any decisions that make the total expenditures exceed total revenues in the original approved balanced budgets or increase the debts as compared with the original approved budget. In case a decision is made in violation of the preceding provisions, the People's Congress or the government at higher level should order a change or annulment of the decision.

According to the proposal of budget adjustments for 2007 submitted to the provincial People's Congress by the Yunnan province, with approval of the 5th Session of the 10th People's Congress, provincial budgetary expenditure of the first half of 2007 was 18 billion Yuan, but in the implementation of the budget for various reasons, the financial resource available was more than the number expected at the beginning of the year, and the budgetary expenditure required an opportune adjustment. After careful studies, the provincial government made a proposal of budget adjustments for 2007 and submitted to the standing committee of the provincial People's Congress for examination and approval.

The proposal made clear that the source of funds for budget adjustments and among the expenditures appended to the provincial budget, 1.48 billion Yuan would be arranged for projects of infrastructure, economic development, and environmental protection; 570 million Yuan would be arranged for spending of social security and health care; 650 million Yuan would be used for agricultural development and disaster prevention; 350 million for maintaining stability and administrative construction; 660 million for education, and science and technology; and 140 million for other expenses. Such a proposal of budget adjustment enables the provincial People's Congress to fully understand the intent of budget adjustments of the provincial government and facilitates future supervision over the implementation. The report finally explained the reason why adjustment in 2007 was more than the previous years and pointed out the direction of future work.

The Jiangxi provincial government submitted to the standing committee of the People's Congress explanation for Proposal of Provincial Budget

Adjustment in 2010 (Draft). The first part explained the reasons and basis for budget adjustments and the second part clarified the main contents of the budget adjustments: (a) Revenue budget adjustments: According to Management Measures for Bonds, Budget of Local Government in 2009 of the Ministry of Finance (Financial 2009 No. 21), bonds revenues of local governments are to be fully included in the provincial budget. On the basis of the budget at the beginning of the year, an additional 6.5 billion Yuan of debt income was added to the revenue budget. (b) Expenditure budget adjustments: On the basis of the budget at the beginning of the year, an additional 6.5 billion Yuan was added to the expenditure budget.

The report of the budget adjustment in 2010 submitted to the standing committee of the People's Congress by the Hubei province also fully explained the reasons for the adjustments and specific elements and clarified provincial budget adjustments: (a) The provincial revenue budget adjustments: the provincial total financial revenue was adjusted to 117,811,470,000 Yuan from 109,211,470,000 Yuan with an increase of 8.6 billion Yuan of debt income. (b) The provincial expenditure budget adjustments: the total provincial expenditure was adjusted to 117,800,190,000 Yuan from 109,195,890,000 Yuan with an increase of 8.6043 billion Yuan in which (1) The provincial general budget expenditures were adjusted to 27,424,130,000 Yuan from 26,045,060,000 Yuan with increase of 1.37907 billion Yuan. The main items which were subject to adjustment were as follows: (a) Expenditure arranged for bonds income of the local governments was 1.37477 billion Yuan. (b) Expenditure for issuing domestic and international debts was 4.3 million Yuan. (2) Transfer payment was adjusted to 90,376,060,000 Yuan from 83,150,830,000 Yuan with an increase of 7.22523 billion Yuan of debt-lending expenditures. The last part proposed strict management of bond funds and made suggestions for effectively preventing the risk of debt policy.

According to these practices, the system of supervision over provincial budget adjustments by the People's Congress in China is relatively unified and normative. Various provincial governments report in detail the overall proposal of budget adjustment and related measures in policy in accordance with the laws, facilitating the provincial People's Congress to fully understand and supervise the implementation of the adjustment proposals.

Chapter 3

Problems in the Process of Budgetary Supervision of Provincial People's Congress

The power of budgetary supervision of the provincial People's Congress is authorized by the Constitution. However, as the Constitution incorporates few conceptual provisions, and its specific laws have limited principle regulations; it makes the power of budgetary supervision of the provincial People's Congress merely procedural and not substantive. Lack of substantial effect of budgetary supervision reflects the constitutional problems. The constitutional principle of budget require members of the society to participate and supervise public financial activities. Yet the reform of budgetary system in China overemphasizes government control of the budget and ignores the democratic supervision of the budget, thus, forcing the grass-root governments to gradually solve the problems in the legal system. The current budgetary supervision system in China is not ideal. For example, at the provincial level, the representatives of the People's Congress generally feel more confused about its supervision powers, even though the provinces have made local laws and regulations such as regulations on provincial budgetary supervision in accordance with the spirit of the national budget law.

Section 1. Deficiencies in the Power of Budgetary Supervision

1. The Power of Supervision without Exalted Constitutional Position

The budget is related to operation of the constitutional system. The People's Congress system is an organization of the highest state powers regulated by the Chinese constitution and whether the system runs well or not closely relates to comprehensive development of the Chinese constitutional system. Budgetary supervision is an extremely important part of the powers vested in the People's Congress. The Chinese political system is quite different from western separation of powers. The difference determines that supervision of the People's Congress over the government is one-way mode i.e. without any power to veto the People's Congress.

The system of the representative agencies to limit the powers of the government urgently needs improvement. The accountability mechanism has not yet been established so as to prevent People's Congress from punishing the illegal budgetary behaviors of government leaders through a relief system at the constitutional level. Although Supervision Law has regulations on inquiry and recall; the exercise of the power of budgetary supervision in accordance with these regulations is not justified by the provisions of the Constitution. Especially in Chinese political system, this becomes an important field for researchers to study on how to really protect constitutional authority of the power of budgetary supervision of the People's Congress.

With the economic and social development, local governments are earning enormous revenue. In this process, some areas develop abnormally fast and the number of government employees expand so quickly that the cost of maintaining social stability keeps rising. This in return leads to a lot of debts on local government. Although China's provincial government shoulder heavier political responsibility, the leaders of the government have much more financial resources and it seems that the boundaries of its powers are getting increasingly blurred. A surge of non-budgetary income and irrational increase of governmental investment make it more difficult for the People's Congress to supervise the government. A comprehensive legal system of budgetary supervision should have all financial revenues and expenditures of the government supervised by the People's Congress and make the citizen clearly understand its public services.

The allocation of financial resources between the People's Congress and the government is kind of a decision-making and implementation relationship, which requires the People's Congress to actively exercise their powers to ensure that the government is supervised completely. Unfortunately, with the practice of financial powers, budgetary supervision of the People's Congress has seriously been weakened, as the strong administrative powers broke the balance of the power between legislative and executive. Budgetary supervision stresses that the representative agencies can supervise the entire government financial revenues and expenditures and ensure the budget is transparent, approved-in-advance and restricted-in-the-process.

But budgetary supervision suffers from system deficiencies such as cursory budgetary compilation, large scale of non-budgetary funds and dispersive management of budgetary revenues and expenditures. The governments were not even allowed to submit comprehensive and detailed budgets to the People's Congress before the reform of departmental budget.[1] The Constitution, Law of Organization of the Local People's Congress and Government, Supervision Law, Budget Law, and Audit Law all stipulate that the local People's Congress and its standing committee supervise the government's implementation of budget. Nevertheless, the People's Congress cannot make substantial supervision over government budget and sometimes are actually ignored and as a result the constitutional power of budgetary supervision is being weakened.

The governments regard financial budgets as pure administrative powers and always insist on supervising it themselves. As a result, the governments maintain monopoly in information of financial revenues and expenditures, rarely taking their initiative to disclose information or reporting implementation of the budgets, not to mention releasing it to the people. Article 18 of Supervision Law states that the government departments should fulfill their obligations of providing all aspects of information, but due to the administration-centered system characteristics, the supervision departments can hardly get access to budgetary information.

2. Narrow Space for the Operation of System

China is a large nation with a single institution where various areas greatly differ. In the financial game between the central and local governments,

---

[1] Ren Xi-rong. Systematic Analysis of Growth of the Budget Supervision Power of the Local People's Congress: An Example of Constitutional Development in China. *Jilin University Social Science Journal*, 2010, (7): 92.

the central government often relies on financial transfer payments to maintain financial or regional balance. China's budget law clearly provides that financial transfer payments should be included in the budgets and Article 5 of the Budget Law enumerates that the budget of local government should include revenues turned over by the lower level governments and revenues refunded or subsidies granted by the upper level governments. Article 19 of Regulation for the Implementation of the Budget Law also cites similar requirements. It shows that both the central government's transfer payments to the provincial government and provincial government's transfer payments to the lower-level government should be included in the provincial budgets.

In reality, however, violations of the requirements in various provinces is very common. The No. 12 audit announcement released by the National Audit Bureau on June 13, 2010 shows that, in four provinces, the budgetary reports of central transfer payments made by the financial departments are incomplete. To make local budgetary compilation complete, the Ministry of Finance began to inform the expected number of special transfer payments from the central government since the end of 2008 and ordered the local governments to accordingly compile and report budgets. Audit investigation shows that although management and use of central special transfer payments were in line with national requirements, the number of transfer payments informed by the Ministry of Finance was not completely included in the budget for 2009.

In reality, the transfer payments for local governments will neither be supervised by local audit departments nor by National People's Congress as it is not included in the budgets. In particular, the total scale of the central transfer payment is determined after implementation of the central budget of current year and will be paid to the local governments in new fiscal year, which makes provincial financial departments unable to have the transfer payments included in the budget of current year; leading the local People's Congress unable to effectively supervise.[2] In this context, the space of budgetary supervision of the People's Congress is significantly narrowed down. Generally speaking, the financial transfer payment

[2] Xu Yang-guang. *Legal Analysis of the Financial Transfer Payment System*, Beijing: Peking University Press, 2009: 154–155.

system overemphasizes how to address the existing financial imbalance, while ignoring standardization of the financial relations between the governments and necessity of its legal adjustments.[3]

Lack of clear division of revenues and expenditures between governments causes deviation of the budgetary implementation. Such uncertain factors as central special subsidies and tax rebates have great impacts on compilation of budget. In the process of making the budgets, the Ministry of Finance is yet to inform the lower governments about the specific numbers of the special subsidies or tax return. Furthermore, the central government always releases and adopts new policies so that the local governments have to adjust their budgets — causing the issues of frequent changes of budgetary implementation.[4] Consequently, the provincial People's Congress can only exercise its insubstantial power of supervision as it hardly obtains financial information.

The CCP maintains political leadership, which is prescribed in the Constitution. Even in the fiscal fields, the Party grasps important powers of making decision. While taking part in the budgets, the People's Congress must treat legal relationship with the standing committee of the Party in order to truly fulfill the substantial function of budgetary supervision on behalf of the civil society. The Party committee has substantial impacts on the budgetary supervision of the People's Congress through two basic approaches: One is to have meetings of the standing committee to make principal decisions in advance for the financial budgets. Actually most of the leaders of the People's Congress were former members of the standing committee of the Party Committee at the same level and they did not have enough motivation to modify the resolutions passed by the standing committee of the Party Committee. And the other is that the standing committee of the Party Committee penetrate its intent into the Party group of the People's Congress through internal discipline and traditions of the Party.

At present, the procedure of the budgets in many areas is designed as follows: the financial departments develop the draft budget; the leaders of

[3] Xu Meng-zhou, Ye Shan. On System Arrangements of the Financial Transfer Payment Between Governments. *Social Sciences*, 2010, (7): 69.

[4] Zhu Jin. Local People's Congress Budget Supervision: Status, Problems and Solutions. *Yangtze River Forum*, 2008, (6): 57.

the government hold meetings to review and make decision; the government then submits it to the People's Congress for examination; and the People's Congress eventually passes it. Once a decision has been made by the Party Committee prior to the supervision of the People's Congress, in China's political system and the context of the political standpoints of the cadres, generally it is very difficult to modify the decision in the draft budget. Moreover, the main leaders of the People's Congress possibly have taken part in the decision of the draft budget, and then the leaders of the government actually has known that the People's Congress does not propose amendments to the budget, thus ignoring the requirement that the draft budget must be submitted to the People's Congress for examination a month in advance in accordance with the Budget Law. This turns the power of budgetary supervision of the People's Congress as null.[5]

In recent years, the provincial Party secretaries in China generally undertake the position of directors of the standing committee of the provincial People's Congress. In the general election before the first meeting of the Tenth National Congress in March 2003, almost all provincial Party secretaries in every provinces were recommended to be candidates of the directors of the People's Congress; except a few provinces where the provincial Party secretaries were members of the political bureau. Presently, the provincial Party secretaries are the directors of the People's Congress in most provinces. Accordingly, during elections of many cities and counties throughout the country, the Party secretaries are recommended to be the directors of the standing committee of the People's Congress.

The reason why it is generally required to recommend the provincial Party secretaries as candidates of the directors of the provincial People's Congress is that in 2002 in the report of the 16th National Congress the concept of governance by law was brought forward for the first time. The report of the 16th National Congress clearly pointed out that according to the principles of considering comprehensively the overall situations and coordinating all the relationships — it needs to regulate the relations between the Party committee, the People's Congress, The National Committee of the Chinese People's Political Consultative

[5] Ma Jun. *Chinese Public Budget Reform: Rationalization and Democratization*, Beijing: Central Compilation and Translation Press, 2005: 67–68.

Conference (CPPCC), and civil communities supporting the People's Congress to fulfill the functions of a state power organ in accordance with law. This helps in turning the wills of the Party into the wills of the nation through electing the candidates recommended by the Party to be the leaders of the organs of state power.

3. Imperfect Organization of the People's Congress System

Due to no representative election in a true sense from the central to the local, the structure of the members of the People's Congress at all levels is not ideal. In the eyes of common citizens, the People's Congress is the place for retired cadres or leaders having no bright political future. As mentioned earlier the main leaders of the provincial People's Congress mainly come from retired leaders and the associate directors are generally retired provincial leaders. The financial sources of the People's Congress in China is not completely independent as good amount of funds come from the government at the same level and the salaries, wages, welfare and treatment of the staff of the provincial People's Congress in many provinces are given by the original units, which also to a great extent causes them unable to boldly supervise the government departments. Besides, in China, the Party governance is overwhelming and the deputies to the People's Congress only have the rights of routine voting in the few days of meetings which are very short, as there is no permanent representative system.

Furthermore, the system of identifying the deputies to the People's Congress in China is based on the quota of proportion. Most of the deputies have no efficient professional skills and there are no specialized support institutions or assistants for the representatives of the people and members of the standing committee of the People's Congress. For this reason, the People's Congress is unable to truly and thoroughly carry out supervision over the budgetary implementation. In particular, it seems that the local People's Congress has a tendency to remain constrained by the local officials and lose political resources due to monopoly of the local political elite.[6]

---

[6] Pan Zhao-min. Analysis Impacts of Structural Changes on Supervision Efficiency of the Deputies to the Local People's Congress. http://www.fepc.org.cn/Article.aspx?ArtID=245.

Professional incompetency and lack of energy for fulfilling their duties are major problems which the deputies to the People's Congress must face during supervision of budgets. Generally speaking, there is no approach for them to participate in budgetary supervision during the recess. Even some of members of the standing committee of the People's Congress are part-time officials. According to the researcher's surveys on the percentage of full-time members in the standing committee of the provincial People's Congress, the highest is 69% in Shandong province, and the lowest is in Jiangsu, with only 23.3% and the average percentage of the 30 provinces is 46.6%. Lack of professional ability of the deputies to the People's Congress and high percentage of part-time members lower the effectiveness of supervision, while it surely raises the cost of supervision. Since many deputies and members of the standing committee are officials of the Party or the government, their position do not allow them to spend much energy or interest in supervision of the People's Congress.

In addition, as the amateur or part-time deputies have no time to gather political information or seldom exercise the right to make recommendations for other national state organs or have no strong awareness of representative — it is difficult for them to inquire the government officials in the meeting to carry out effective supervision. Actually, professional diversity should not be taken into account and government officials should not be the deputies to the People's Congress as well.[7] According to the characteristics of representative system, only regional and demographic factors should be taken into account as the principle of proportion of members of the People's Congress.

The department in the People's Congress which fulfills the function of supervision of budgetary implementation is generally the financial and economic committee of the People's Congress, as budget committee is not set up in most provinces. The department's functions range from examining the plans for national economic and social development to making financial regulations and carrying out budgetary supervision. To solve problems and issues, some provinces are looking for an eclectic scheme,

[7]Zou Ping-xue. On Professional Deputies to the People's Congress. Fudan *Political Science Review*, Institutional Structure of Democracy in China, Shanghai: Shanghai People's Publishing House, 2008, 6: 57–60.

i.e. to set up a budget working committee (budgetary supervision office) under the standing committee of the People's Congress, but apparently, this is not enough as the budget working committee is just an office of the standing committee of the People's Congress and it can only provide advice to the standing committee. Its nature, status, and duties are quite different from that of the specialized budget committee that should be set up in the People's Congress.[8]

Section 2. Insufficient Transparency of Budget Information

1. Specific Results and Causes

Fiscal budget information is the basis for all financial supervision. A budgetary supervision system can normally run on the basis of the precondition of full information disclosure. After tax-sharing reform in 1994, provincial financial management in China became significant. Accordingly, reform of provincial fiscal management system is also increasingly gaining urgency and provincial budgets have an extremely important political and social significance. However, the current budget information disclosure system and budgetary supervision system do not go hand in hand, and it will be necessary to explore a system platform for information disclosure of provincial budget and really have governments' capacities of public governance recognized and supervised by the public. The present situation is that the power of budget information disclosure is held by the governments and consequently they can determine when and how to disclose it. Furthermore, there is no institutional design for communication and collection of the public opinions between the public and government after disclosure.

Communications of budget information between provincial People's Congress and government are not smooth. In developed countries, the government and representative institution often negotiate on budget issues face to face. The People's Congress cannot really act as representatives of the public in supervising public budget funds if it does not take part in the process of compilation and implementation of budgets. Budget process is

[8] Xu Shu-na. On Budget supervision of the People's Congress. *Studies on Several Major Issues about Draft Amendments to China's Budget Law*, 2009: 173.

quite transparent such as compilation, examination, voting, passing and even approval or rejection of the president. Although the procedure is complicated, every step is ensured to be open and transparent and normally the government is required to disclose budgetary implementation and accounting information in various ways so as to turn invisible government into visible government. Currently in China, there is information asymmetry between the government and the People's Congress. This serves as the primary reason for imperfect budget information disclosure and audit report system and lack of effective fiscal information sharing system.[9]

The relationship between China's local government and the People's Congress is typically shown in this way: Every time on the People's Congress session, the government just provides the deputies to the People's Congress draft budget in brief and withdraws it after the meeting in the name of confidentiality. Most deputies to the People's Congress can neither understand government budget information nor can they provide any professional advice, not to mention supervision and decision making. The relationship between the People's Congress and the government over budget information determines that the People's Congress cannot substantively supervise budget. China's Budget Law stipulates that financial departments of government at all levels should have the main contents of draft budget submitted to standing committee or special committee of the People's Congress for preliminary examination one month before the session. As most of the local governments prepare it in a short time and draft budget is always delayed, the deputies just get the budget reports during the People's Congress session, making it difficult for the deputies to perform a complete comprehensive, exact and profound examination and supervision. Furthermore, China's budget vote is a pass-after-one-vote way and there is no debates in the process, thus leading the deputies to fall into a dilemma in which they neither completely veto nor express their opinions even if they doubt some of the contents of the draft budget.[10]

[9] Zhao Wen. *Concise Reading of Budget Examination and Supervision of Local People's Congress*, Shanghai: Fudan University Press, 2008: 154–159.

[10] Liu Wei. On the Path of Improving the Budget Supervision System of the People's Congress. *The People's Congress Research*, 2008, (1): 17.

Public Policy Research Center of Shanghai University of Finance and Economics in 2009 and 2010 respectively evaluated China's information disclosure of provincial finance and drew a conclusion that provincial budget information disclosure in China is not good and the legal foundation is not solid. In the investigation report of 2009 quantitative analyses were made on transparency of general classification of provincial government funds, government transfer payments, government assets and liabilities, social security fund, state-owned enterprise fund, and so on. The report came to a conclusion that financial transparency in China was not qualified on the whole even though it was evaluated with a lower standard and it was quite far from the target of guaranteeing citizens' right to know.[11]

Transparency of classification of the government funds in various provinces show that the scores are low on the whole and the overall situations greatly differ, reflecting certain institutional characteristics of the transparency of government financial information disclosure. In contrast to Fujian, Anhui and Beijing, many provinces provided little information on general government fund revenue. It obviously violates the basic principle of financial transparency where budgetary compilation, implementation, and reporting should be disclosed. This principle not only requires budgets to be disclosed in a comprehensive framework but also requires the government to provide the main reasons for budget arrangements. The investigations of fiscal transparency in various provinces show that some provinces do not follow the basic requirements of fiscal transparency to disclose their budgetary compilation and implementation, let alone providing the budget basis. In this case, the public or the taxpayers are unable to know the usage of the funds by their trustees i.e. the governments.[12]

The evaluation report made by the center in 2010 pointed out that (1) the governments have taken poor initiatives in information disclosure and there is little substantive information disclosed on the

---

[11] Jiang Hong. On Budget Transparency Study. Studies on Several Major Issues about Draft Amendments to China's Budget Law. *Symposium of the Major Issues about Amendment to Budget Law*, 2009: 164.

[12] Hong Jiang. *Report on China's Financial Transparency: Assessment of Provincial Financial Information Disclosure*, Shanghai: Shanghai University of Finance and Economics Press, 2009: 101–102, 131–133.

governments' official websites or in publications. (2) Although China has made some progress in government information disclosure in the past years, it still does not match with the political and economic developments in China.[13]

The current system of budget information disclosure in China is imperfect with very weak legal base and poor access to budget information. There are few laws on budget information disclosure and in these limited laws and regulations the requirements of integrity and validity of budget information disclosure are not sound or operational in practice. It will pose an immense positive impact on budgetary supervision in various provinces if the government can gradually improve system construction related with information disclosure, starting from demands of budgetary supervision information in practice, spreading good samples of some provinces, and gradually popularizing it throughout the country.

In current Budget Law, fiscal information disclosure is not paid full attention. The First Article of the General Provisions stipulates that the law is enacted in accordance with the Constitution and for the purposes of strengthening the distribution and supervisory functions of budget, improving the budget management of the State, intensifying the macro-control of the State, and ensuring sound socio-economic development. In this article, the State is regarded as the main body of management and supervision while the relationship between the government and the People's Congress is neglected.

It essentially emphasizes the regulation and supervision of executive branches of the government over its affiliated agencies, units and individual behaviors. The function of representatives of the People's Congress on supervision depends on sufficient information of budget and complete, accurate, timely and specific understanding of the source, and use of public funds and assets.[14] Therefore, there is a long way to go before making regulations on budget information disclosure, and practical laws

---

[13] Liu Xiao-Bing, Deng Shu-lian, Wen Jiao-xiu. The Evaluation of China's Provincial Fiscal Transparency in 2010. *Shanghai University of Finance and Economics Press*, 2010, (6): 56.

[14] Jiang Hong. On Budget Transparency Study. Studies on Several Major Issues about Draft Amendments to China's Budget Law. *Symposium of the Major Issues about Amendment to Budget Law*, 2009: 50–56.

and regulations of budget information disclosure should be made in accordance with the guideline principle of public, exception of private to clearly define the principles, procedures, scope, requirements and legal liabilities of information disclosure.

2. The Consequences and Influences

As for the government, failure in institutionalization and legalization of budget information disclosure would make the civil society unable to supervise the government accordingly and will also prevent the government from providing the civil society with truly efficient and fair public services. A highly centralized and lack-of-restraint-government inevitably has no initiatives to disclose budget information and its public policy decisions will lack credibility and authority. Without strict supervision over the revenues and expenditures the government puts across the self-interests and preferences of some leaders as guidelines of action. Such a government will not be trusted by the public and is indeed an invisible government.

All government revenues should be supervised by the civil society but currently local governments have a lot of non-budgetary revenues[15] and a large number of local governments rely on land finance. A great amount of fiscal revenues from selling land become the main part of public finance, but unfortunately it is not supervised by the civil society. Experts believe that the Budget Law enacted in 1995 is too rough and the regulations on non-budgetary funds are too general, making it free of supervision. It runs in the opposite direction from financial and political democracy.

If democracy fails, all government behaviors against public expectations will likely gain popularity. Constructions such as office buildings, hotels, and even airports have become projects of showing political performances by some local leaders and the most powerful government

[15] I am not in favor of the concept of non-budgetary income, because the nature of all income is the same, i.e. public budgets. The so-called non-budgetary income refers to the part of dark funds that are not included in the budget and not supervised by the public. Their existence is not ensured by any legal reason. The currently popular concept is just borrowed here.

departments seize the best areas to build the most luxurious office buildings and even in suburbs they build a variety of training centers, conference centers, and reception centers with fiscal resources of hundreds of millions. The fiscal resources are used without any supervision of the People's Congress. This implies that the civil society cannot participate in public decision-making and political democracy would be impossible without disclosure of budget information.

If disclosure of budget information stays at a rather low level, it would be difficult for the public to accept authority of public decision-making and it would also be difficult to inspire public passion for participating in public governance so as to provide the government with more intelligent support. Besides, authoritarian, opaque governments have more trouble in obtaining revenues than transparent governments, thus, facing more trouble in forming solid financial foundations for their public governance. This will also lead to an increase in cost for making tax policy due to communications.

If the government initiatively discloses budget information or discloses it in response to citizens' application, the government behavior will be effectively regulated. Rent-seeking opportunities will reduce and at the same time it can also promote the transformation of government functions from the privileged authority into service institutions by laws. The government who does not have transparent financial information available to the civil society will increase opportunity costs of governance due to corruption and make it difficult to control efficiency and integrity of civil servants. The government will eventually lose credibility among the public and even lead to unreasonable establishment of government agencies. Black-box operations will definitely lead to unharmonious relationship between the government, the market and the enterprises. Asymmetry of information and rise in costs of governance will also become prevalent.

Section 3. Imperfect Procedure of Budgetary Supervision

1. Unreasonable Design of the Procedures

In terms of the laws and politics in practice, China carries out a system dominated by the guidance of the Party, which determines most important affairs of the government. Public policy like budget will be discussed by the Party committee before administrative decisions. By the time the People's Congress intervene in the draft budget, it has already come into effectiveness with little room left for modification. Furthermore, when the People's Congress is informed that the Party committee has passed the budget, they are less enthusiastic to supervise it. Moreover, local government seldom submits the draft budget to the People's Congress for examination before a month in advance. The Budget Law does not provide effective regulations on legal effectiveness and approaches for preliminary examination of the People's Congress.

China currently lacks a legal system that can control the process of the budget at the very beginning that includes detail of the budget, information disclosure, budget adjustment, and budgetary implementation. This leads the People's Congress to always participate in supervision at the final stage, thus failing to find problems on time. Furthermore, the People's Congress does not pay enough attention to legislative investigations after the reform of the government budgetary system, failing to improve early-stage budgetary supervision system. The People's Congress also fails to enhance configuration of its own budgetary supervision institution and staff, so as to get out of the plight where information is asymmetric. Therefore, the People's Congress cannot fully integrate the supervision into the process of budgetary compilation.

The budgetary supervision includes three stages: pre-supervision, mid-supervision, and post-supervision. Most of the laws in China focuses on pre-supervision while neglecting mid-supervision and post-supervision, which needs more professional knowledge and techniques, and common deputies to the People's Congress are not qualified.[16] Since 1995, according to the Audit law and Interim Measures for Audit and Supervision over the Implementation of Central Budgets, the provinces have developed relatively simple local regulations on audit and supervision over budgetary implementation, expect defining the relationship between the audit departments and the People's Congress in the supervision.

---

[16] Liu Xiao-bing. Improve the Status of the Audit Department, Implement the National People's Congress Budget Supervision. *Shanghai University of Finance and Economics Press*, 2008, (3): 52.

According to the current legal system, for three reasons the People's Congress only indirectly guides the audit department, which cannot carry out independent supervision under the political environments in China, since audit department is affiliated to the government at the same level.[17] Firstly, audit is not independent. According to the current administrative system in China, the audit department is an internal part of the government. Secondly, the scope of audit is too narrow and execution power of audit is greatly restricted. Thirdly, the audit process is not completely open.

2. Limited Latitude for Procedural Operation

In the Budget Law, provisions on the power of budgetary supervision of the People's Congress are not detailed enough. How the People's Congress amends the draft budget when it examines and approves the budget is not very clear. In addition, the local People's Congress has limited capacity in obtaining budget information and therefore, cannot make budget amendment. That is the reason why budgetary supervision of the People's Congress is weak.

The long-standing administrative mode dominated by the Party committee makes the People's Congress lack sufficient means and information for controlling public finance, thus failing to establish legal authorities. The legal characteristics of the budget determine that its implementations must be supervised. The Constitution and Budget Law establish the legal system of supervision, which, in practice, is flawed on several occasions, as the budget powers are exclusively controlled by the government. The fundamental reason lies not in the budgetary system but in the operating mechanism of the Chinese constitutionalism. Chinese Budget Law did not expect the draft budget to be vetoed by the People's Congress, and consequently it did not provide the legal responsibility and counter-measures for the vetoed draft budget.[18]

---

[17] Ren Xi-rong. Systematic Analysis of Growth of the Budget Supervision Power of the Local People's Congress: An Example of Constitutional Development in China. *Jilin University Social Science Journal*, 2010, (7): 92.

[18] Wang Shi-tao. Constitutional Analysis of Chinese Finance. *Journal of Gansu Politics and Law College*, 2008, (2): 8–13.

The relevant laws in China provide general regulations on supervision of financial transfer payments but lack specific operational procedures. In practice, the Law of Financial Transfer Payments is yet to be enacted and therefore, the People's Congress finds it difficult to carry out effective supervision. The State Council and the financial department of provincial government naturally become the authoritative departments of implementing financial transfers, leaving room for flexible use by the government. In such a circumstance, the rights and responsibilities in financial transfer payments are not clearly prescribed, the provincial People's Congress really cannot carry out comprehensive and effective supervision over the entire process of the budgetary implementation.

Section 4. Case Studies: Shanghai, Gansu and Guangdong Provinces

1. Simplification of the Procedure of Examination of Draft Budget

As the representatives can only pass or reject the budget report as a whole, they will generally follow the suggestions of Financial and Economic Committee of the People's Congress to pass the draft budget, leading the process of examination to be simplified. During the People's Congress session, the deputies can just obtain little information on allocation of the funds. In Examination Report on the Implementation of the Budget for 2006 and the Draft Budget for 2007 in Shanghai, the Financial and Economic Committee of the People's Congress in Shanghai just made a very simple description of the total amount of the financial revenues and expenditures and changes of the proportion without any specific report of analysis.

It made evaluation and recommendations: the Financial and Economic Committee believes that the draft budget for 2007 made by the people's government follows the principles and policies of the Party Central Committee and the State Council. The Party Committee of Shanghai should focus on accelerating construction of the public financial system, deepening the reform, and emphasizing particularly on funds allocated for basic public services. It should also reflect the requirements of scientific development and a harmonious society. After these amendments, the draft budget becomes feasible.

The Financial and Economic Committee recommended the deputies to approve the draft budget for 2007. The consequent Resolutions for the Implementation of the Budget for 2006 and the Draft Budget for 2007 made at the fifth meeting of the 12th People's Congress in Shanghai came to a very simple resolution: the meeting examined Report on the Implementation of the Budget for 2006 and the Draft Budget for 2007, and approved the report as mentioned earlier.

Report on the Implementation of National Economic and Social Development Plan for 2007 and the Draft Plan of Economic and Social Development for 2008 in Shanghai only described the expected amount of the draft budget in figures. It then simply proposed that the draft has been approved by Planning and Budget Examination Committee, who believed that it meets the requirement of scientific development and reflect the principles of the 17th National Congress of the Party, central economic work conference and the ninth Party congress and the third plenary session of Shanghai. The Planning and Examination Budget Committee recommended the deputies to approve the draft plan of economic and social development for 2008.

The consequent resolution was also very simple: The first meeting of 13th People's Congress of Shanghai examined Report on the Implementation of National Economic and Social Development Plan for 2007 and the Draft Plan of Economic and Social Development for 2008 in Shanghai and approved the report. The meeting came to the resolution of approving the budget at the municipal level for 2008 and approving the report mentioned earlier.

The earlier process of budget examination shows that the People's Congress are making more cooperation in examinations of the draft budget rather than making detailed analyses and discussions. It is difficult for the People's Congress to deepen the budgetary supervision. Regulation on Examination and Supervision over the Municipal Budget in Shanghai even does not mention how the People's Congress discusses and votes for the draft budget. Furthermore, the scope of coverage of the provincial budget is relatively narrow and it lacks adequate explanations so that the deputies to the People's Congress can only carry out examination and supervision in form as they are not very professional.

2. Inability to Veto the Use of Specific Budgetary Funds

While examining draft budget for 2004, the deputies to the People's Congress of Guangdong Province questioned the departmental budget of 36 million Yuan for the provincial Party committee and official kindergartens and the third group of the deputies also questioned the proposal of the provincial financial department. At the meeting of the deputies to the People's Congress in 2005, in examination of the draft budget of the government, the deputies felt unsatisfied when they found the funds allocated to an official kindergarten rising to 15 million from 14.7 million Yuan in 2004. Several deputies pointed out that the official kindergartens do not fall into the category of public finance.

However, as China Youth Daily reported, Draft Budget for 2011 of the Provincial Departments in Guangdong Province showed that financial allocations for eight affiliated kindergartens in Guangdong reached up to 68.63 million Yuan in 2011. In these eight official kindergartens, Guangdong provincial talents training kindergarten obtained 24.04 million Yuan, and even the kindergarten of the science and technology department got 1.59 million Yuan. The Draft Budget showed that the budgets covered five types of expenditures on these kindergartens: General expenditures in 2011, expenditures of wages and benefits, expenditures of goods and services, expenditures of personnel and household allowances, and other capital expenditures.[19]

Huang Ping, the director of the budgetary supervision office of the Financial and Economic Committee of the People's Congress in Guangdong Province made response through media that these kindergartens were public institutions and the budget itself was not inappropriate. However, a commentary of the People's Daily published on January 26, 2011 held that publicity was one of the basic attributes of public finance. The services provided by public finance should be shared and all citizens should have equal opportunity. In some areas, the official kindergartens are not public but designated, that is to say, they only recruit the children of the leaders or staff of the organs, or at least the children of the organs have priority, which in reality is to turn public funds into welfares for a

[19] 'Official Kindergarten Supported by Finance' will Continue to Exist or not. *China Youth Daily*, 2011, 2(2).

small portion of people. The phenomenon of official kindergartens supported by public finance is unfair in two ways: firstly, it is unfair for the public and their children and secondly, it is also unfair for the private kindergartens.[20]

The comment of Beijing News made on January 29, 2011 could more accurately reflect the dilemma of the current provincial budgetary supervision system. The comment pointed out that according to the survey, majority of people thought that the official kindergartens supported by public finance in Guangdong Province, which exclusively take in children of the leaders of the governmental offices are unreasonable. Although the deputies severely questioned it, the eight kindergartens of Guangdong provincial government obtain the funds without any changes. Why?[21] As there are no regulations on vote and amendments to specific funds arrangements in the budgetary supervision system, the provincial People's Congress cannot separately vote for specific budget funds, or it will be embarrassed by vetoing the provincial budget as a whole due to unreasonable financial allocations for the kindergartens.

3. Vacuum in Supervision in the Process of Budgetary Implementation

On September 30, 2010, Gansu provincial audit department released on its official website, "Audit Report on Implementation of the Provincial Budget and Other Financial Revenues and Expenditures in 2009 in Gansu Province."[22] This is a very typical case of provincial budgetary supervision. On October 13, Gansu official website released a news report entitled, "Audit Results of the Implementation of the Gansu Provincial Budget came out: 11 Key Projects 'Saving' 88.8 Million Yuan," and made comments on the audit announcement released on September 30.

---

[20] Official Kindergarten is the 'Tail' of Planned Economy. *People's Daily*, 2011, 1 (26).

[21] Why Official Kindergarten Cannot be "Get Rid of"? *Beijing News*, 2011, 1 (29).

[22] Auditing Report on Implementation of the Provincial Budget and Other Financial Revenues and Expenditures in 2009 in Gansu Province. Gansu Provincial Government Official website, 2010, 9 (30) (Accessed on October 12, 2010).

A report from *Gansu Daily* also published on the Gansu governmental website a comment entitled, "Audit Results of the Implementation of the Provincial Budget in 2009," showed it is generally good, but abuse of special funds cannot be ignored. It held that the results show, implementation of the provincial budget and other financial revenues and expenditures is generally good. Financial revenues and expenditures kept increasing and financial expenditures were focused on livelihood of the people. However, abuse of special funds still exists. On October 14, a commentator named Zhao Feng issued on Xinhua website an article entitled, "How can the Audit Report Ignore Major Issues in Budgetary Implementation." The author pointed out that the announcement revealed several major problems in the budgetary implementation.

As for some outstanding issues the announcement just described in a few words without detailed elaboration, making the public doubtful. According to the announcement, ten units such as the Gansu provincial highway bureau withheld 260 million Yuan of funds for site and station construction, the department of education and student loan management center withheld 53.13 million Yuan of surcharge for education and compensation for student loan risk and 590 million Yuan of share transfer income of the Hua Coal Group by the provincial state-owned assets supervision and administration commission was not turned over. Thousands of million or even billion Yuan of funds were abused, the amount was quite huge and the problem was quite serious, but all of them were treated lightly in a few words. The audit report is not the only document treating the issues in this way and Gansu is not the unique province. There are no details or explanation for abuse of the budget funds and state-owned capital operation income which the public are most concerned about in the final audit announcement, directly turning clear audit into confused results in the eyes of the public.

In part of the announcement discussing audit of the implementation of the Gansu provincial budget, the provincial departments held that it seriously implemented the macro-control policies and further improved the principle of the budget revenues and expenditures, but in the implementation of the budget and asset management problems still exist, especially in the second or third levels of the departments. While discussing misappropriation, abuse and withholding special funds in Article 6, it pointed out that three departments of the agriculture and animal husbandry and its subordinate animal husbandry central stations abused 4.64 million Yuan of agricultural special funds; four departments of the provincial highway and transportation authority bureau abused 24.13 million Yuan of station construction funds for building command center, purchase of office.

According to the regulations on the responsibilities of budgetary supervision of the local People's Congress in Supervision Law, the standing committee of the provincial People's Congress is granted the power to supervise similar key funds and the power to question and dismiss the officials. In accordance with the requirements of the Supervision Law, the People's Congress of Gansu Province on July 26, 2010 passed Enforcement Measures for Supervision Law in Gansu Province. Article 20 provides the key contents that standing committee of the provincial People's Congress should supervise and grant the standing committee of the People's Congress the power of supervision over budgetary implementation. As to significant events or emergence of major issues in the budgetary implementation, the local people's government should promptly report to the standing committee of the People's Congress.

The standing committee of the People's Congress can require the people's government to instruct the audit department to specially audit the major issues in budgetary implementation concerning the reform, development, overall stability and vital interests of the people or the public concerned most and to review the special audit report. The standing committee can require the financial and economic committee of the People's Congress or financial and economic working office of the standing committee to keep supervising the key issues reflected in the audit report and then report the results to the standing committee. In accordance with relevant regulations of the Supervision Law, it further improves the terms of exercising the dismissal power, making the law more practical. However, such a system would likely fail to put it into effect due to lack of accountability mechanism or power relief.

Vacuum in supervision over the process of budgetary implementation reflects necessity of more legal provisions for the People's Congress' initiative participation in supervision. Article 13 of the Budget Law grants the standing committee of the provincial People's Congress the power to supervise the implementation of the provincial budgets and Article 18 of

Supervision Law lists the key contents of budgetary implementation to be examined by the standing committee. But in Regulations on Examination and Supervision over the Municipal Budget of Shanghai made in accordance with the Budget Law, only Article 6 provides the main contents of budgetary implementation to be supervised by the standing committee of the municipal People's Congress rather than ignoring the channels and regulations for the People's Congress' active intervention in budgetary implementation. As Shanghai did not develop detailed specifications for supervision over budgetary implementation following the Supervision Law, the People's Congress which is not politically powerful eventually gives up supervision.

Enforcement Measures for Audit and Supervision over the Implementation of Local Budget in Guangdong Province promulgated in 1995 only has 14 articles and does not mention the relationship between the People's Congress and the audit department in the budgetary supervision and only Article 4 generally points out that audit of the local budgetary implementation should facilitate the people's government at all levels to know the financial revenues and expenditures and other financial funds. This will help to strengthen management of the financial revenues and expenditures; facilitate the standing committee of the People's Congress at various levels to supervise implementation of the local budget and other financial revenues and expenditures; facilitate the financial and taxation departments at all levels and other departments to effectively function in budget managements and promote legalization of the supervision over the local budgetary implementation, and audit and supervision of other financial revenues and expenditures.

Regulation on Audit of Budgetary Implementation in Guangdong was passed on the eleventh meeting of standing committee of Guangdong People's Congress on January 16, 2009. It is not difficult to find that with the influence of the Supervision Law changes occur to the legislative ideas in the relationship between the People's Congress and the audit department. Especially Articles 17, 18, 19 are consistent with the legislative thoughts of the Supervision Law with more detailed terms for implementation, making the relationship between the People's Congress and the audit department closer in the process of supervision over the government budgetary implementation. If there are further accountability mechanisms and rights relief measures, the supervision system will play a more substantial role.

Chapter 4

The First Part of System Improvement: Rational Allocation of the Power of Budgetary Supervision

Section 1. The Power of Supervision in Budgetary Decision-Making

1. Balance between the Powers of Budgetary Decision-Making

In the budgetary process, the provincial People's Congress needs to begin supervision from the stage of making decisions for the budgets so as to balance various budgetary powers and ensure to exercise the power of budgetary supervision at the very beginning. Firstly, there should be no priority and difference of weight in the power of making budgetary decisions. If the People's Congress cannot express opinions at the very beginning of the budgetary decision-making, it will be unable to maintain balance of the powers of making budgetary decisions, and would thereby be hardly able to carry out supervision in the budget process.

Secondly, the People's Congress should always participate in all kinds of meetings relating to budgetary decisions and express their opinions on time as a basis for budgetary decision-making. For instance, as the standing committee of the provincial Party committee is gathering ideas for the provincial budget, all the members of the standing committee of the provincial People's Congress should attend the meeting and fully express their opinions. Avoiding such a situation would lead to the People's Congress unable to interfere with the budgetary decision-making once the standing committee of the Party committee has made the budget.

Thirdly, the People's Congress should deal well with the relation with the government in the process of making budgetary decisions and budgetary compilation, organizationally establish statutory communication channels with the government for exchange of opinions, and set up a special internal agency to communicate with the government to ensure timely exchange of opinions on the draft budget. Only in this way can the People's Congress build a solid foundation for exercising the power of budgetary supervision in the whole process of the budget.

Budget reformers usually hope to reconstruct the budgetary system, including budget structure, procedure, and rules, on which the participants rely when they make a decision on allocating the funds. The budget structure involves the form of distribution of the powers and responsibilities of various participants in the budget process. The budget reforms failed to achieve the desired results and the key reason is that the reforms neither really changed distribution of the powers nor fundamentally changed the decision-making patterns of the budget participants in the budget process.[1] This implies from another perspective that the basis of legal reform of budgetary supervision is the balance of powers and rights. The legal platform of budgetary supervision of the People's Congress can well function as expected on the basis of comprehensive balance mechanisms and sound organization of supervision.

2. Standardization of the Power of Budgetary Decision-Making

The People's Congress must uphold the Party's leadership. The leading Party group of the provincial People's Congress shall fully play a leading role in the congress, while the leading Party group in the congress should well coordinate with the standing committee of the provincial Party committee. It enables the provincial People's Congress to participate in the budgetary decision-making process of the provincial Party committee and in the meantime better regulate exercise of the power of making budgetary decisions of the Party committee. The provincial Party committee will not necessarily make budgetary decisions in one meeting.

---

[1] Ma Jun. Politics of the Budget Reform in China: Achievements and Plight. *Journal of Zhongshan University (Philosophy and Social Science)*, 2007, (3): 68.

It can discuss it in several stages for good exchange of ideas with the People's Congress each time, enabling the People's Congress to fully play the major role of the professional supervision agency in gathering opinions on the draft budget.

The Party committee does not fully grasp the details of public financial revenues and expenditures since they are generally not involved in government management. However, the Party committee has the highest decision-making power. In addition to the Party secretary and the governor, the provincial deputy secretary, executive vice governor, and a few of the vice governors who are in charge of economic, financial, and industrial development are also the members of the standing committee. As they powerfully control the financial budgets in the fields that they are in charge of, the standing committee of the Party can generally determine a province's financial arrangements while the government to a large extent is just an executor. Therefore, it is very important for the People's Congress to supervise the standing committee of the Party over the budget and it needs to strengthen top-level design of an effective supervision system in this field.

To enhance the power of budgetary supervision of the provincial People's Congress, it is necessary to regulate exercise of the budget powers. In terms of the actual process of supervision of the People's Congress, it will be impossible to ignore the relationship between the People's Congress and the Party committee in supervision, as the Party committee maintains close relations with the administrative departments of government. To supervise the powers of the administrative departments, the People's Congress needs to regulate the powers of making budgetary decisions of the Party committee. The ruling Party leads the institution of state powers while the People's Congress supervises implementation of the policies of the ruling Party in accordance with the laws, featuring the budgetary supervision in China. To correctly handle the relationship between the leadership of the Party and the supervisory powers of the People's Congress, it needs to build a reasonable budgetary supervision system for the People's Congress in which one of the important stages is to reorganize the budgetary procedure.[2]

---

[2] Zhu Jin. Local People's Congress Budget Supervision: Status, Problems and Solutions. *Yangtze River Forum*, 2008, (6): 58.

With the development of China's democratic politics and legal construction, the budgetary supervision system needs to be improved by facilitating the People's Congress and the government to avoid the failure of the overview and coordination functions of the Party committee, integrating the leadership of the Party with the powers of the People's Congress in accordance with the laws. The government under the leadership of the Party committee often has the supreme authority, restricting the ability of budgetary supervision of the People's Congress. The decisions of the leaders of the Party and the government are irrevocable as they jointly discuss and determine most of the administrative affairs and then release documents, including financial issues such as additional funds for annual key investment projects of the government, social public services, and construction of public infrastructure.

However, the provincial Party committee is not quite familiar with the specific use of the funds, and its decisions are mostly based on considerations of macro-factors with less importance for the proposal of budget adjustment Public opinions need to be taken into full consideration in the highest decision-making so that the financial budget decision-making of the Party committee will be scientific and rational, preventing the leaders of the Party committee from expecting more allocation of funds for the departments that they are in charge of, thus showing performance for the entire financial budget funds instead and making it easier for the People's Congress to supervise the budgetary implementation.

If the Party committee and the government lack a comprehensive strategic plan that is highly binding, and guiding allocation of the funds, the leaders will play a very important role in the process of fund allocation. Currently, the Chinese provincial budget operates under a fragmented authoritarian system. Although the situations in various provinces differ, almost all the leaders can somehow influence the allocation of funds. Most importantly, the powers through which they influence allocation of the funds are informal budget powers.[3] Since the Party committee in principle has the power of making decisions, it should not make the final

---

[3] Ma Jun, Niu Mei-li. Reconstruction of Chinese Public Budget System: The Power and the Relationship — Based on Researches of Local Budgets. *Observation of China's Development*, 2007, (2): 14.

decision for a budget just after single discussion. It should invite the People's Congress to take part in the process of making the budget decision in several stages, figuring out a draft resolution and submitting it to the standing committee of the People's Congress. Then the People's Congress will review it and gather public opinions or ask specialized institutions to evaluate the draft budget and give recommendations for improvement, which can be referred to in the following discussions, thereby improving precision and consistency of decisions of the standing committee of the provincial Party.

As in many financial fields, since supervision of the government by the People's Congress is not possible, the financial budget powers of the government need to be regulated to make more room for the People's Congress. Since 1949, the national budget has been a single form of financial revenues and expenditures with all the funds included in the same budget table, regardless of the nature and allocation of funds. Such a budget which is relatively simple and concisely reflects the overall feature of the financial revenues and expenditures, is suitable for the financial system of unified revenues and expenditures in the past. According to the Regulation on National Budget Management of the State Council in 1991, the government would adopt multiple budgetary systems from 1992, classifying the financial revenues and expenditures into two categories — the usual budget and the constructive budget — in terms of different economic natures. Regulation on the Implementation of the Budget Law passed in 1995 further classifies the budget into the government public budget, the state-owned assets management budget, the social security budget and other budgets, making the budget more scientific. The Budget Law passed in 1994 makes explicit regulations on the basic principles of budget management, the levels of budget management, the budget organization system, budget year, budget management powers, the scope of budget revenues and expenditures, budgetary compilation, examination and approval of the budget, budget adjustment, the final accounts, supervision, and other aspects.

Thus there was significant progress in the budgetary legislation. The budget accounting system started to be improved since the ministry of finance initiated the Total Financial Budget Accounting System, the Enterprise Accounting Standards, and the Administrative Department

Accounting System in 1998, strengthening the foundation of budget management. The State Council has also strengthened the management of non-budgetary funds and has made Decisions on Strengthening Management of Non-budgetary Funds in 1996 to strictly define non-budgetary funds as financial capital, requiring the departments to report the plans of non-budgetary revenues and expenditures. The State Council proposed a basic management mode, separately managing the revenues and the expenditures and guiding the basic direction for non-budgetary funds management. The ministry of finance correspondingly developed supplemental documents such as Measures for the Implementation of Non-budgetary Funds Management and Interim Regulations on Management of Special Account of Central Budget Funds. It makes the government budget powers more normative and scientific and gives more room for development of the power of budgetary supervision of the People's Congress.[4]

3. Coordination between the People's Congress, the Party Committee, and the Government

The political system under the Party leadership is a basic principle of China. As the representative of the general Party committee, the standing committee of the Party Committee usually performs daily decision-making powers. In the budgetary decision-making, provincial budgets are generally discussed and determined by the standing committee of the provincial Party committee, following the central economic work conference and the actual requirements of local development. The standing committee of the provincial Party committee will certainly require the financial departments to prepare the technical draft budget (scheme) and submit it to executive meetings of the provincial government, which in turn submits it to the meetings of the standing committee for examination.

After validation, the standing committee will pass it to the People's Congress for formality examination. The problem of this procedure is that

[4]Ren Xi-rong. Budget Supervision and Financial Democracy: Growth of the Power of Budget Supervision of the People's Congress. *Journal of University of Political Science of East China*, 2009, (5): 104–105.

before submission to the People's Congress, the Party committee has already made a decision. The director of the standing committee of the People's Congress usually is the general secretary of the provincial Party committee, who has participated in the discussion on the draft budget of the standing committee of the Party committee. Once the Party committee has made decisions for the budget, the Party members in the People's Congress usually do not want to express their opinions against the Party committee. Furthermore, even if the standing committee of the People's Congress or the deputies to the People's Congress point out some problems existing in the individual budget expenditure of the government, the government will generally refuse to accept the opinions with the excuse that the Party committee is in agreement.[5]

The Constitution of the CCP provides that a leading Party group shall be set up in a central or local state organ, people's organization, economic or cultural institution, or other non-Party unit. The group plays the critical role of the leadership. Its main tasks are to implement the Party's line, principles, and policies; discuss and decide major issues in its unit; control cadre management; unite with non-Party cadres and the masses in fulfilling the tasks assigned by the Party and the State; and guide the work of the Party organization of the unit. Article 47 provides that the composition of a leading Party group is decided by the Party organization that approves its establishment. The group shall have a secretary and, if necessary, deputy secretaries. A leading Party group must accept the leadership of the Party organization that approves its establishment. Under this provision, the members of the group are not elected by the Party congress but designated and led by the Party committee approving establishment of the group. The leading Party group in the standing committee of the People's Congress is a hub joining the Party and the People's Congress. The Party always influences and controls the People's Congress through the internal channels of the leading Party group in the standing committee of the People's Congress.[6]

---

[5] Ma Jun. *Chinese Public Budget Reform: Rationalization and Democratization*, Beijing: Central Compilation and Translation Press, 2005: 68.

[6] *Ibid.*, p. 70.

The People's Congress shall not only uphold the Party's leadership, respecting the budgetary compilation power of the Party, but also coordinate the relationship between the People's Congress, the Party committee and the government. First of all, it should fully play the role of the leading Party group of the People's Congress. Smooth communication with the provincial Party committee is the foundation for the People's Congress to strengthen supervision in the process of budgetary decision-making. It needs to ensure that the Party members of the People's Congress and members of the standing committee of the provincial Party committee have equal powers in budgetary decision-making or in introducing debate and voting mechanisms, thus achieving budgetary democracy in the Party first. Second, the leading Party group of the People's Congress also needs to strengthen communications with the leading Party group of the provincial government, collecting more public opinions to guide the budgetary decisions of the provincial government to avoid irrational decisions made by the provincial government due to information asymmetry or incompleteness of information.

According to the local laws and regulations of various provinces, the provincial People's Congress is expected to exercise budgetary supervision from points of view of local economic and social development. However, in terms of the legal responsibility, the People's Congress lacks measures to truly balance the government as the government officials cannot be truly dismissed because of the budgetary responsibility by the People's Congress. The election or nomination system of the candidate members of the People's Congress and its standing committee also has significant impacts on the supervision incentives of the People's Congress. Chinese politics is featured by the relationship between the standing committee of the People's Congress and the provincial Party committee when nominating the candidates of the standing committee of the People's Congress. Although theoretically the representatives of the people should be elected from the people, the members of the standing committee of the People's Congress are generally retired leaders from the Party committee and the government at the same level who will neither be against the successive leaders of the Party nor have impetus to supervise the government as their treatment and funds are controlled by the local Party committee and the government.

Budgetary supervision is very professional work with sophisticated techniques while the deputies to the People's Congress are not with fixed terms. Besides, most of the representatives lack professional financial knowledge and so do not have enough energy and ability to supervise the budgetary decision-making and its implementation. On the contrary, they often exercise their power of voting annually in a rash manner. Although, the standing committee of the People's Congress has relatively more time and energy to carry out supervision, as most of them are former government officials, they will not have too much interest in budgetary supervision. Besides, as they are still regulated by the disciplines of the Party, they often either consciously or unconsciously retain only behaviors that are consistent with the Party and eventually give up ideas which seem to be inconsistent with the disciplines of the Party. Therefore, the People's Congress can substantially play the role of budgetary supervision only by making full use of democracy in the leading Party group, by improving the budgetary voting system of the People's Congress and fully underlining democracy in the budgetary decision-making process.

Section 2. Power of Supervision in the Process of Making Budget

1. Supervision over Amendment to the Draft Budget

In the modern public budget, the power of preparing a budget is held by leaders of the government. The budget will be submitted to the congress for examination after checking by leaders of the government. The main powers of budgetary decision of the representative agencies include examination and approval of the government budget. The power of amendment to the draft budget is a derivative of the powers of public financial decision and the power of supervision. In terms of the laws, amendment to the draft budget is a sort of proposal put forward by the representatives of the people for the government budget plan. It is one of the statutory powers of the representatives of the people and is an extremely important procedure for the representative agencies to exercise their financial powers. Therefore, an indicator to measure the power of a congress is whether or how the congress can amend or modify the draft budget submitted by the government. It can be said that the power of amendment to the draft budget is the core of the budgetary powers of a modern congress.[7]

At present, there is neither regulation on the amendments to the draft budget for the Chinese National People's Congress nor legal practice in the strict sense. Nevertheless, the local People's Congress has already made some regulations on budgetary amendment and created some cases, with no further rules and norms. Due to the composition of the representatives and the limited time of the meetings, amendment to the central draft budget is not currently feasible, but in recent years, some of the provincial People's Congress has made progress in the practical exploration of the budgetary reform with some regulations or decisions on entitling the deputies to the People's Congress to the power of budgetary amendment. Since the tax-sharing reform in 1994 in China, the relationship between the financial power and the administrative power of the central and local governments is not very smooth as a large number of non-budgetary funds disrupted the budgetary management system. With the enhancement of the democratic awareness of the citizens, their insistence of budgetary supervision over the government by the local People's Congress is growing.

The legal significance of the budgetary supervision of the People's Congress mainly refers to the power of supervision entitled to the congress as a power organ in the process of making, examining, and approving the draft budget and implementing the budget. Amendment to the draft budget belongs to an examination procedure of the draft budget after compilation. From the legal perspective, it can be inferred that the power of amendment to the draft budget of the People's Congress needs clearly regulate the normative procedure of amendment. First, it needs to solve the foundation of the budgetary amendment, including expanding the discussing and preparing period, examining the budget relatively independently from budgetary amendment, and providing sufficient information for budgetary examination and amendment.[8] Procedural regulations should regulate

---

[7] Ma Jun, Lin Mu-hua. Budget Amendment Powers of the Modern Parliament. *Calls for the Public Budget*, Beijing: Central Compilation and Translation Press, 2008: 96.

[8] Zeng Jun-ping, Shang Hai-quan. On Budget Amendment. *On Problems of Draft Amendment to the Budget Law of China,* 2009: 152–158.

communications between the budgetary compilation departments, the People's Congress, and its departments in the entire budgetary examination process. On the other hand, it needs to solve problems such as debate and voting procedures, and decision-making rules at the meeting of the representatives.

Development of budgetary democracy determines the direction of the entire political reform and has a significant impact on the political position of the People's Congress and the entire political power structure. True implementation of the powers of amendment to the draft budget needs to seriously consider the relationship between the People's Congress and the ruling Party. Granting the People's Congress the power of budgetary amendment will have a significant impact on the political power structure. In fact, the political position of the People's Congress in the existing political system needs to be redefined.[9] Improvement of the budgetary examination and supervision system is indeed a problem of political system rather than a technical issue, which cannot be totally solved by the revision of the Budget Law.

In fact, allowing the People's Congress to amend the budget does not mean that the People's Congress has absolute power. In terms of the use of public funds, similar to the government officials, the representatives or congress members may also have tendency of predatory opportunism. In order to benefit some interest groups or for other considerations, the deputies to the People's Congress have no less incentive to spend public funds than the government officials do.[10] In fact, in the countries throughout the world where the budgetary supervision system of the People's Congress is relatively perfect, the power of amendment to the draft budget is strictly constrained. In improving the power of amendment to the draft budget, there is a need to strengthen not only the power of budgetary supervision of the People's Congress, but also the design systems to prevent the budgetary power of the People's Congress from expanding, avoiding too much interference into the executive powers, thus lowering efficiency of the government.

---

[9] Xin Shaowen. Rigid Budget Constraints, the First Step of Restricting the Powers of the Government. *South Reviews*, 2010, (2): 35.

[10] Zeng Jun-ping. The Budget Amendment Rights Need Strict Rules and Norms. *Journal of Shanghai University of Finance and Economics*, 2008, (3): 54.

2. Strengthening the Power of Amending the Draft Budget in the Stage of Preliminary Examination

From the perspective of combination of the public choice theory and constitutionalism, the decision-making mechanism that the public choice system relies on has inherent flaws, as the government agencies and officials may abuse public powers, illegally seek private interests, and operate with low efficiency. Therefore supervision over the decision-makers is very important. Exercise of the powers of amendment to the draft budget is a sort of effective supervision over the public financial decision-making mechanisms and the budget powers of the government. The system of checks and balances between the power agencies is necessary to improve the fairness and effectiveness of the public financial expenditures. Budgetary compilation is an entrusted agency behavior between the citizen and the government. It needs to establish a complete and effective supervision mechanism as there are various risks.

The public interests are discovered and confirmed in the discussion and approval of the budget by the representative agencies. The representative agencies debate, hear, modify, read, vote, and approve the draft budget submitted by the government to continue to look for maximum public interests and the representatives and political parties express their willingness reflecting the requirements of each class or group and the public interests are eventually confirmed by the final approval of the budget.[11] Compilation and approval of the budget is essentially not only talking about simple list of numbers, report summary, or items but comparison and selection of different potential public expenditures regarding conflicts between the public interests, private interests and local interests. Budgetary implementation is not a simple spending of financial funds as it reflects the implementation of public policies and the achievement of public benefits.[12] Therefore, the People's Congress has the power to amend draft budget of the government on

[11] Jiao Jian-guo. Budget Mechanism Theory: Analysis from the Economic, Political, Legal, Financial and Decision-making Perspectives. *Journal of National Institute of Public Administration*, 2002, (4): 79.

[12] Zhu Da-qi. On the Purpose and Principles of Revision of the Budget Law from the Nature of State Budget in China. *China Law*, 2005, (1): 81.

behalf of the citizen, which is not only the requirement of theoretical supervision mechanism but also the substantive procedure to promote social welfare.

Although scholars express the power of amendment to the draft budget in different ways, they recognize importance of the power to a great extent and somehow propose specific ways to exercise the power. The Constitution and the Local Organization Law clearly stipulate that the People's Congress has the power of amendment to the draft budget. During the People's Congress session, presidium of the congress, special committee, or representatives with joint signature can put forward amendments to the draft budget. The revision of the Budget Law should expressly grant the People's Congress the power to amend or even reject the draft budget in accordance with the Constitution and the Local Organization Law.[13] It is hard to say that the Constitution and Local Organization Law expressly define the power of amendment to the draft budget. Nevertheless, the deputies to the People's Congress are really deprived of such a power.

China's Budget Law and other relevant laws and regulations do not grant the People's Congress the power of budget amendment, which is a bottleneck constraining the People's Congress to play the role of supervision in the budgetary process. As there is no budget amendment power, the People's Congress only has two options: to reject or pass the draft budget as a whole. In the Chinese political system, rejection is neither realistic nor necessary, while complete approval can prevent the People's Congress from substantively exercising its power of budgetary supervision. Therefore, in the revision of the Budget Law in the future, the People's Congress needs to be granted with the power of amendment to the budget.[14]

But strictly speaking, in practice, the provincial People's Congress has made many attempts to amend the government draft budget. Provincial laws and other regulations on budgetary supervision have tried to define

---

[13] Zhao Wen. Research Reports on Local People's Congress Budget Examination and Supervision. *Condensed Reading of Local People's Congress Budget Examination and Supervision*, Shanghai: Fudan University Press, 2008: 179–180.

[14] Ma Jun, Lin Mu-hua. Budget Amendment Powers of the Modern Parliament. *Calls for the Public Budget*, Beijing: Central Compilation and Translation Press, 2008: 100.

the power of amendment to the draft budget, or at least mentioned the concept of the power of amendment and there is no contradiction with any higher laws, only lack of constructive regulations and operational measures. In 2003, one of the deputies to the People's Congress in Guangdong province proposed to the government to add an additional item of the expenditures. Although it was not successfully submitted to the general assembly for voting as the presidium of the People's Congress refused it, it was undoubtedly the first attempt to exercise the power of budgetary amendment of the People's Congress.

The Budget Law only provides that the draft budget is compiled by the administrative department and is examined and approved by the People's Congress. But it does not explicitly say that the People's Congress has the power of amendment to the draft budget or whether the government has the power of checks and balances regarding the examination and approval of the budget. In terms of budgetary management in practice, the People's Congress actually only has the power to approve or reject the draft budget. The powers of making fiscal policies of the provincial government in China are more than the power of supervision of the People's Congress. If the People's Congress is entitled the power of amendment to the draft budget, the budgetary duties of the power agencies can be strengthened. On the other hand, unreasonable budgetary expenditures can be constrained in an additional way. Even if the budget is examined and approved by items, it is impossible to examine each specific item and so the power of amendment to the draft budget is necessary for the People's Congress to coordinate the relationship between the People's Congress and the government.[15] The People's Congress needs to be granted reasonable budgetary powers to control the powers of making decisions and supervising the budgets of the government on behalf of the people following the requirements of the principle of financial democracy. Revision of the Budget Law should expressly grant the People's Congress the power of amendment to the draft budget and the corresponding power of balancing the government in order to promote democracy in budgetary compilation and examination and

[15] Liu Jian-wen, Xiong Wei. On Development and Improvement of China's Budget Law. *Administrative Law Review*, 2001, (4): 8.

strengthening the role of the representatives of the people in budgetary examination.[16]

During the People's Congress session, the departments and individuals who have the right to make proposals under the general legal framework can propose to amend the draft budget, which are the inherent requirements of the People's Congress system. However, at present, the People's Congress basically examines and approves the draft budget through a comprehensive approach. There are no strict regulations on budgetary amendment in the Budget Law and in other relevant laws and regulations. Although the comprehensive examination and approval system has advantages like increased efficiency of decision-making, in such a system, the People's Congress can play only a limited role in budgetary supervision. As the critical budgetary power of a modern congress, the power of amendment to the draft budget is the power to protect the purse. It is put forward to ensure reasonable use of public funds. More fundamental protection is needed to support the power of amendment to the draft budget of the People's Congress.[17]

The Constitution, People's Congress Organization Law, and the Budget Law neither provided detailed regulations on amendment to the draft budget by the People's Congress nor explicitly defined such a power. The deputies to the People's Congress have the right to make a proposal and in the People's Congress session the deputies do have the right to propose to amend the draft budget, even though the draft budget amendment is not simply a power to vote and it needs follow-up political consultation. If there are no specific regulations, it will be difficult for the deputies in the given time of the People's Congress session to pass the draft budget after collecting all the opinions. Furthermore, it needs a consultation system for the budget before the People's Congress session or the People's Congress needs hold special meetings to debate on the draft budget to validate the annual budget, which goes beyond the current academic argument whether the power of amendment to the draft budget is necessary to be designed in the current People's Congress system.

---

[16] Liu Jian-wen. Constitutionalism and Chinese Financial Democracy. *Tax Research*, 2008, (4): 6.

[17] Zeng Jun-ping. The Budget Amendment Rights Need Strict Rules and Norms. *Journal of Shanghai University of Finance and Economics*, 2008, (3): 54.

In terms of examination of the budget, in fact, it is no longer a purely "checks and balances" between the legislative and administrative powers as it involves the interests of various social communities and interest groups. The representative agency is not only the legislature but also the department collecting public opinions and whether they have the power to amend the budget or not is an important issue to be considered in the constitutional laws of many countries. Attribution of budget power and the balance mechanism between the executive and legislative powers are closely related with democracy and constitutionalism in a country.[18] In addition, viewed from the logic of constitutional decentralization, the power of budgetary examination controlled by the congress is a critical system setting in the principle of separation of constitutional powers. The power of budgetary examination is just one of the traditional powers of the congress to control the government. It becomes a constitutional system which is absolutely necessary as the financial and economic measures and actions of the government must be approved by the congress. The government is under the direct supervision of the people in order to reach the goal of a reasonable and moderate spending, and eventually protect human rights through the principle of separation of powers and checks and balances.[19]

The first proposal of the provincial draft budget amendments came out at a meeting of the 10th People's Congress in Guangdong Province. The provincial government financial budget for 2003 was composed of 11 items, including insurance funds such as unemployment, pension, and child birth while basic medical insurance funds was not mentioned. Some deputies to the People's Congress held that as the basic medical insurance was a part of the social security system, they proposed to add the item of basic medical insurance funds to the provincial government fund budget. Finally, the presidium of the general assembly made a resolution: the budget amendment proposal made by 11 deputies led by Liao Xiao-ying from Guangzhou delegation was not submitted to the assembly for examination as the provincial government had no right to set up insurance funds, which should be done by the State Council.

---

[18] Zhu Kong-wu. *On Financial Constitutionalism*, Beijing: Law Press, 2006: 206–261.
[19] *Ibid*., pp. 124–125.

Although the amendment proposal was not eventually submitted to vote, it did imply that many deputies began to substantively pay attention to the financial expenditures of the various government departments. In fact, in many other provinces such as Zhejiang, Hunan, Hubei, and Shanghai, as there are no regulations on the power of budgetary amendment, the People's Congress many times suspends its work in examining the government budget and the local People's Congress in some areas finally took the measure to vote the major financial expenditures separately in advance. This phenomenon reflects the importance and urgency of the power of draft budget amendment, therefore, Chinese laws should provide the People's Congress and the government more room to reach consensus on budgetary amendment in the process of examining and approving the budgets.

In the process of making budgetary decisions in reality, the People's Congress needs enough time to examine the draft budget and needs a statutory organ to examine and amend the draft budget in a statutory procedure. Paragraph 2 of Article 37 of the Budget Law provides that the financial departments under the government of the province should submit the main contents of the draft budgets one month before the sessions of the People's Congress for preliminary examination to the relevant special committee of the People's Congress, or to the relevant working committee of the standing committee of the People's Congress in accordance with the decisions made by the council of chairmen of the standing committee of the People's Congress. Yet, it is difficult as the legal position of the department in charge of preliminary examination is not clear, the contents to be examined are undefined, the legal results of examination are unknown, there is no participation of experts, the preliminary examination intervenes in budget approval too late, and the statutory time for preliminary examination cannot be guaranteed.[20]

Since China has an administrative centralized government, major decision-making of the provincial governments in general are subject to the major decisions of the central government. As a result, although the provincial budgetary compilation starts in July and August, all the provinces

[20] Liu Jian-wen, Xiong Wei. Reform of Budget Examination and Approval System and Improvement China's Budget Law. *Jurist*, 2001, (6): 55.

have to hold financial meetings after the central economic work conference and the State Council economic work conference at the end of the year. At that time, although the government budget has not yet been submitted to the People's Congress, as for the departments, the budget has been basically completed. In order to implement the policies of the central government, the provincial government will usually maintain some funds, which will be used to adjust the budget after the economic work conference and it will be submitted to the People's Congress after the consent of the provincial Party committee. It will be obviously too late for the deputies to the People's Congress to take part in examination of the budget during the People's Congress session when the budgetary compilation has been finished. Therefore, the legal status of the preliminary examination of the draft budget needs to be strengthened, and it should be ensured that the deputies to the People's Congress participate in early budget draft discussions, thus changing the current situation that only the budget committee of the standing committee exercises the power of preliminary examination.

As to the examination of the draft budget, the professional capacity of examination of the deputies to the People's Congress is also an important factor. Among the deputies to the People's Congress, the proportion of Party members, administrative leaders, and principal officials of the government departments is too high, thus making it difficult for them to play the expected professional role in the examination of the draft budget. Also, they are unable to express negative views in their related work. Besides, the People's Congress session is very short and the representatives have to pay main attention to examine a variety of other reports.[21] The draft budget is always submitted to the deputies near the end of the meetings. In addition, the information is insufficient with low transparency, and due to information asymmetry of the budget and lack of professional competence, it is more difficult for the deputies to fulfill their responsibility. Therefore, the People's Congress must set up a specialized assistance mechanism to allow the People's Congress to take part in the examination with the support of the society, avoiding hasty participation in the final

[21] Ma Jun, Hou Yi-lin. Policy Process and Budget Process of Provincial Budget in China: Surveys in two Provinces. *Economic and Social Systems Research*, 2005, (5): 66.

vote of the budget due to lack of professional examination, thereby turning preliminary examination of the budget into a mere formality, and finally making the deputies exercise an extremely important power of budgetary supervision by voting even without full understanding of the draft budget.

Section 3. Sound Restrictions on the Power of Budgetary Supervision of the People's Congress

1. To Avoid a Trend of Opportunism of the Power of Budgetary Supervision of the People's Congress

The budget is the result of private property delivery to the government from the civil society with the aim to provide public services for improving the people's livelihood. Therefore, as the representatives of the civil society, the People's Congress naturally undertakes the duty of supervision over the budget, which is compiled and implemented by the public financial departments of the government. To some extent, although both the representative agency and the government department are representatives of the civil society, they undertake different duties and functions. The People's Congress cannot completely replace the government in financial configuration. Due to deficiency of organizational structure and professional competence, the provincial People's Congress in China is unable to fully exercise its power of supervision. It will be very dangerous if the government is given powers in decision-making without enough energy and preparation to exercise them. The objective of the power of budgetary supervision of the People's Congress is to collect more public opinions for the government, leading the government to be more cautious and simultaneously comprehensive in making decisions for arrangement and spending of the public funds.

Furthermore, any kind of power in modern politics has its limits, and unrestricted power will become an obstacle of improvement of the livelihood of the civil society. As to the budget, the government may have opportunistic behaviors, which should be regulated and limited by some representative agencies such as the People's Congress. However, the People's Congress and other representative agencies are made up of people who are rational economic men, which means that the legislative departments may also be opportunistic in the budget process.[22] Therefore, in terms of the integrity, the improvement of the budgetary system actually needs to solve issues of the third level: To impose constitutional constraints on the People's Congress to prevent it from opportunistic behaviors in the budgetary decision-making. Constraints on the power of budgetary supervision of the People's Congress can be divided into active and negative constraints to both bind the People's Congress to fulfill its duties and stop it from excessive action.

The power of budgetary supervision of the People's Congress is not only an important power but also a major legal responsibility as it is an indirect power of control with the ultimate goal of ensuring financial democracy and administrative efficiency. There will be trouble if the People's Congress freely adds or deletes items of the government draft budget proposed by the. Therefore, enhancing the budgetary power of the People's Congress does not mean absolute power transferred to the People's Congress and its standing committee, since the legislative is composed of representatives on behalf of various areas who are apt to consider their local interests, especially passing the expenditure bills in support of their local interests. Besides, they may turn to seek other representatives' reciprocal support to pass the budget proposal concerning their local interests. So the expansion of public expenditures is inevitable. In advancing the process of budgetary democracy, there is a need for further strengthening of the power of budgetary supervision of the People's Congress and the design of some kind of mechanism to restrict the People's Congress in order to control the scale of financial expenditures and improve efficiency.[23]

2. Rational Allocation of the Power of Budgetary Supervision of the People's Congress in the Constitutional Framework

Rational configuration of the financial powers and the operation restriction mechanism is the economic and legal basis of sound operation of a country's political powers. The reason to clearly define the financial

[22] Zeng Jun-ping. The People's Congress Budgetary Decision-making, Opportunistic Behaviors and Constitutional Constraints. *Journal of Shanghai University of Finance and Economics*, 2009, (2): 48.

[23] Ma Jun. *Chinese Public Budget Reform: Rationalization and Democratization*, Beijing: Central Compilation and Translation Press, 2005: 83.

power, have a limit on it, and carry out strict supervision is that the national financial power is an important part of the state power and the basis of public affairs management of the national agencies. It is related to the national legislative power and is the basis of rule of the law system. As the financial power can influence the official functioning of other state organs or affect the motivation of the state officials, there is configuration of the national financial powers to prevent power of a certain state organ from over-concentration.[24] Positive constraints on the financial power need a practical system to guarantee that the people could urge the People's Congress to exercise its power of supervision. What is more, it also needs a rational system to prevent the People's Congress from abusing its powers. Therefore, the improvement of the budgetary supervision system is closely related to the electoral system of representatives of the People's Congress. If the voters cannot elect the deputies to the People's Congress who can truly represent their own interests, the fundamental rights of the civil society will be weakened by a bad system.

Constraints on the power of budgetary supervision of the People's Congress should be strengthened and finalized by the constitutional system in order to avoid compilation, implementation, and adjustment of the budget using legislative and executive powers. Some scholars have proposed that the budget opportunistic behavior is prevalent not only among the government representatives but also among the members of the legislative organs. For example, in order to win in the election campaign or for other considerations, the legislators, possibly irresponsibly, expand the scale of the budget. It is absolutely necessary to impose constitutional constraints on the total expansion since the legislative organs are also irrationally opportunistic, causing expansion of the budget scale.[25] Therefore, revision of the Budget Law should ensure that the People's Congress will be able to propose an amendment in the budget by adding expenditures, and should also stipulate specific provisions for proposal of increase of revenues and deduction of other expenditures. It needs to

---

[24] Quan Cheng-xiang. Constitutional Configuration of the State Financial Powers. *Hunan Forum*, 2008, (1): 97–98.

[25] Zeng Jun-ping. The People's Congress Budgetary Decision-making, Opportunistic Behaviors and Constitutional Constraints. *Journal of Shanghai University of Finance and Economics*, 2009, (2): 49.

prevent the People's Congress from making the same mistakes as the government, resulting in increase of burden of the people.

Some scholars also express their different opinions on the budgetary examination boundaries of the People's Congress. The real boundary of negative budgetary examination (reduction) needs definition in the constitutional system. As to the actual boundaries of positive budgetary examination (increase), regulations are needed on the use of financial resources, and the amount added must be constrained by the legislative and supported by related laws.[26] Such a system design is very necessary as it can rationalize the powers between the various representative agencies, preventing them from injuring each other, and enabling the people to eventually enjoy the fruits of the modern political system by truly realizing the rational allocation and exercise of the financial powers under the constitutional framework.

---

[26] Wang Yong-li, Wang Sheng-fang. Boundaries of Examination of Budget Amendments of the Legislature. *Journal of Fujian Management College of Politics*, 2003, (10): 58.

Chapter 5

The Second Part of System Improvement: Strengthening Budget Information Disclosure

Section 1. Improvement of the Budget Information Disclosure System

1. Legal Guarantee of Budget Information Disclosure

Budget is a breakthrough of the political reform in China, especially in the context when local revenues keep growing and the civil society wants to know more about financial situations of the government along with its rapid economic and social development. It is prerequisite to build a government which is limited, responsible and ruled by law. The budgetary supervision system of the provincial People's Congress requires more improvements in many fields in the course of turning to substantive supervision from procedural supervision. Openness and transparency of budget information is the basic institutional guarantee of many budgetary supervision reforms.

The audit results of recent years show that massive corruption comes from the fields where budget information is not open as there is much room for the government to control the financial funds, while the public can neither intervene nor participate in decision-making. In order to fundamentally solve the problem that the government cannot effectively exercise its duties of the representatives — the budgetary supervision of the People's Congress must be based on full understanding of the revenues and expenditures of the government. Yet it is difficult to ensure that the government will open its budget information in accordance with the relevant legal provisions to really promote a smooth transition towards limited government with self-control, and truly protecting the fundamental rights of the citizens.

Budget transparency is far more important than openness in the form of written files. As in full sense the budget not only refers to static budgetary documents, but also essentially is a process of dynamic game. A dynamic game refers to a series of dynamic activities of a statutory body following the legal procedures that includes compilation, approval, implementation, supervision, examination, and final accounts of the budgets. In this process, the most critical point regarding budget transparency is whether and how the People's Congress as the highest speaker of the state powers and providers of public financial funds and authorized representative of the public can dominate the process of compilation, supervision, and implementation of the budget as well as evaluate the performance afterwards. To put it in another way, public participation and supervision in the budget process are more important than disclosure of the budgetary results.[1]

The nature of the public financial funds require arrangement of the government budget to be normative, transparent, scientific, complete, rational, and efficient. Openness and transparency are not only to guarantee the right to know, but is also a standard used to judge whether or not the government decision-making process is normative and effective.[2] The effective budget information disclosure system not only requires the government to take initiative to release the information but also requires the People's Congress to develop a fairly complete regulation system to ensure that people actually supervise, participate, and evaluate the government budget process and that they exercise their powers as masters of the nation as prescribed in the Constitution.

Public budget is the most effective tool for the public to control, supervise, and constrain the government. Openness of financial information is the precondition of the tool and is the most important content with the right to know. The International Monetary Fund (IMF)

---

[1] Zhu Da-Qi. Wish Budget Transparency Improve Further. *Square Round Lawyers*, 2009, (4).

[2] Li Yan. Exploration in Analysis of Budget Transparency from the Perspective of Democratic Supervision. *Journal of University of Central Finance*, 2007, (12): 2.

pointed out in Fiscal Transparency Code that release of financial information should be one of legal obligations of the government and fiscal transparency is a basic principle. The best practice is that the laws require the government to widely disclose financial information to the public and make clear explanations for the exceptions and the reasons.[3]

In terms of the fundamental rights of the citizen, the government budget should be completely disclosed to the society and the public should be allowed to participate in examination and supervision by giving suggestions or criticism in various ways in order to exercise their right to information and right to criticize and make suggestions at constitutional level. Therefore, if the citizens' right to information in financial budget information is not protected by the Constitution, the government will not make the civil society feel satisfied in regard to the disclosure of the financial information.

2. The Requirements of Budget Information Disclosure

1. Completeness. Budget information disclosure must be complete as it does not make sense as long as there are some parts of undisclosed funds. The Organization for Economic Co-operation and Development (OECD) in the report entitled, "Best Practices of Budget Transparency" pointed out that budgets are important government policy documents. The budget should be comprehensive, covering all revenues and expenditures of the government, so that arguments for the alternatives of different policies must be reviewed and assessed. Budgets including related documents should provide detailed description of each item of the revenues and expenditures. The budget should contain a mid-term planning in order to clarify the plans of at least next two years after the current fiscal year and the trend of the revenues and expenditures. Similarly, the current budget proposals should be basically consistent with the earlier vision in the financial report with detailed explanations for each significant deviation.

[3] Jiang Hong. *Report on China's Fiscal Transparency: The Evaluation of Provincial Fiscal Information Disclosure*, Shanghai: Shanghai Financial Press, 2009: 47.

Some scholars have summarized the explicit attribute of budget transparency as the basic requirements of modern public budget. Budget transparency has many features, at least including the following: (1) it opens the division of work between government and market; (2) opens government organizational structure, and their functions; (3) open the government's budget target and the bases of budgetary compilation; (4) open all information of the revenues and expenditures of the government; (5) budgetary process is open and transparent; (6) make all explanations for the budget comprehensible; (7) budget information within fewer files is more available to the public to check it out.[4]

This shows that budget information disclosed by the government should be complete. Furthermore, not only various budgetary reports and statements of the government, but also the explanations for the budget, preliminary assessment and forecast made by the government are complete, and performance of implementation of the budget in the past is available to the representative agencies and the civil society for reference. Completeness is an important principle of budgetary compilation and is the basic requirement of fiscal transparency. With the information, the legislative and the public can understand all the activities of the government, compare different acts for making choices, analyze success and failure, and evaluate performance of the government.[5]

In general, financial activities of the government can be divided into general management, trust, and investment activities. Accordingly, financial funds of the government are divided into general funds of government, trust funds, and public enterprise funds. The principle of completeness requires disclosure of financial information covering these three funds. The IMF pointed out that the budget documents, final accounts, and other financial reports released by government should include all the budgetary and non-budgetary activities of the government, consolidated financial status, and detailed statements of the government. If financial information of one of the funds is not disclosed, users of the information are unable to

---

[4] Deng Shu-lian. Research Perspective of Standards of Budget Transparency. *Calls for Public Budget*, Beijing: Central Compilation and Translation Press, 2008: 122.

[5] Jiang Hong. *Report on China's Financial Transparency: Assessment of Provincial Financial Information Disclosure* (2009), Shanghai: Shanghai University of Finance Economics Press, 2009: 47.

understand the whole picture of public funds used by the government in operation. A great sum of non-budgetary funds of revenues and expenditures make the local government hesitant to open budget information. This attitude was prominent, especially over the past decade when real estate industry were booming and profits from land selling became a major financial source of the local government. The aim of non-budgetary fund runs in the opposite direction counter to the public budgetary system as this part of the funds will inevitably be out of control by the People's Congress and spent arbitrarily by local governments.

2. Standardization. Budget information disclosure does not mean that disclosure or even full disclosure can truly meet the requirements of the public. It seems that the public would still be confused if the government does not disclose the budget information in a normative way. If the information is disclosed in very general and disordered terms, the representative agencies and the public cannot effectively obtain information on collection and use of the public funds. They will then be unable to judge the legitimacy of the sources of the funds or evaluate the performance, as the government can allocate the amount of the funds between different projects. Standardization of the budget information provided by the government means that the government departments should forecast, record, and release financial information with unified and open standards and methods in order to ensure unity, truth, and reliability of the financial information.[6]

Budget information disclosure is not some sort of work which differs much within regions and it should be done with the same national standards. The Ministry of Finance in January 2010 issued Notice on Further Promoting in Information Disclosure of Local Financial Budget to require the local government financial departments throughout the country to normatively and orderly disclose local budget information. According to Regulations on Government Information Openness, citizens, legal persons, or other organizations may, based on the special needs of such matters as their own production, living and scientific, and technological research,

---

[6] Jiang Hong. *Report on China's Financial Transparency: Assessment of Provincial Financial Information Disclos*ure (2009), Shanghai: Shanghai University of Finance and Economics Press, 2009: 52.

request departments of the State Council, local people's government to provide relevant government information. The Notice requires the local governments to seriously consider and handle the applications for financial information disclosure in accordance with the laws and regulations. If the applications are reasonable, related information should be disclosed to the applicants in time.

The financial officials respond in different ways. An official of the financial department of Shanghai said that disclosing the information upon applications is very confusing. Firstly, it's very hard to bind the applicants on openness in dealing with the information as the applicants often release the information to the society. Secondly, how to determine the special needs of production, living and scientific, and technological research is not clearly defined.[7] In general, except the confidential items prescribed by the laws, all financial information shall be disclosed to the public. As to the information which is controversial to disclose, the relevant government departments have responsibility to explain the reason. If necessary, it should be judged in legal procedures. As the government budget consists of so much information that if it is not disclosed in standard and comprehensive way, public will be unable to obtain the information they want.

3. Without delay. The government should release all budget information promptly. They should immediately update and supply budget information in various stages as the budget is not static data statements but a dynamic process of decision-making and implementation. Information disclosure in time is a sort of efficient, honest performance of a government. Especially the representative agencies require a lot of budget information in advance in order to accurately and reasonably take part in supervision over the budget decision-making on behalf of public opinions. Even various departments within the government also need to know the government budget information to improve its management efficiency.

Financial budget actually is a continuous dynamic process with different functions at different stages from compilation to implementation, and

[7] Ministry of Finance Plans to Promote Unified Disclosure of Local Budget. *Jinan Daily*, 2010, 1 (22).

correspondingly the different contents should be disclosed. Before budgetary compilation, the government should release the draft budget and related interpretations. At the same time attention should be paid to the reference data, macroeconomic data, and reports of analysis and assessment so that the financial planning will be fully understood by the public and representative agencies. Furthermore, the government or the People's Congress shall release the reports on assessment and opinions for the government draft budget, that is to say, the interactive process of the People's Congress and the government should also be opened in order to increase public supervision and participation in budget. As long as draft budget is passed, it needs to be released immediately to the public through a legal procedure to facilitate the public to accurately grasp the future financial plans and fully understand the contents of public policies of the government. In the specific process of budgetary implementation, it needs to release without delay the reports of budgetary implementation, key examination and supervision reports of the People's Congress, and audit reports. After budgetary implementation it needs timely disclosure of evaluation information of the performance of the budget funds in order to facilitate the public to compare and expect the contents of the budget for the coming year.

3. Design in System of Budget Information Disclosure

Budget information disclosure has been carried out slowly since 1949 and budget information was even once pronounced as state secret. At the People's Congress session, the departmental budgets and budget information were initially marked secret, to be withdrawn after the meeting, and the budget documents were kept by the head of the delegation, and the deputies had to borrow it from them if they wanted to have a look. Departmental budget does allow the deputies to know how the government spends the money, but the money is spent in such a secret way that it is doubted by the deputies and the public.

From 2005, the labels of Secret were removed one by one and departmental budgets were open to the deputies. In January 2005, the deputies to Sichuan People's Congress participating in the People's Congress session found the label of Secret on the cover of the departmental draft budget removed. In 2006, budgets of 124 provincial units were disclosed to the deputies to the People's Congress in Hunan province. In recent years, each deputy to the People's Congress in Shenzhen is given a copy of departmental draft budget and is allowed to take it home. Simultaneously several provinces and cities began to explore the practice of gradually disclosing the draft budgets to the civil society.[8]

Some provincial and municipal governments have made a bold exploration in budget information disclosure in practice or made commitment of disclosure in the future, with little differences in degree, scope, and focal point of budget information disclosure. Most of the governments began to disclose information starting from budgetary compilation. The methods, time, approaches, and scope of budget information disclosure should be further standardized to make budget information disclosure compulsory. The ways of information disclosure must be institutionalized in practice in order to make budget information disclosure as government's statutory duty.

Budget information can be disclosed through citizens' participation. Hebei province held budget hearings twice in 2004 and 2005. In 2004, information of educational budget arrangements for the next year was announced in newspaper by the government before the hearing and it was attended by representatives of all industries, which played the role of budget information openness. In 2005, in the budget hearing the scope of budget information disclosure was expanded. Provincial departmental draft budgets on agriculture, forestry, and water conservancy in 2006 were disclosed for suggestions of examination. In the hearing, suggestions and recommendations on budget arrangements for direct subsidies to farmers and for science and technology promotion, and technical training were directly adopted.

In April 2010, the officer in charge of Hebei provincial financial department said the scope disclosure of provincial budget in Hebei would be expanded and emphasis would be laid on promotion of departmental budget disclosure, following the practice that total provincial budgets are completely disclosed on main provincial and financial websites. The

---

[8]Tian Bi-yao. China Budget Disclosure Road Map. *People's Congress Research*, 2010, (7): 4.

provincial departments which submit their budgets to the People's Congress for examination should as soon as possible open its departmental total budgets of revenues and expenditures in response to approval of provincial People's Congress. Hebei provincial financial department also strengthened its guidance in budget disclosure of cities and counties in accordance with relevant requirements. It also unified the formats of local financial budget and final accounts report. The budget and final accounts that have been approved by the People's Congress shall be initiatively disclosed to the civil society in accordance with the requirements of being complete and true. As requested, the financial departments at all levels in Hebei province must open budget arrangements, management system, and allocation methods of major expenditures involving people's livelihood such as public education, health care, social security, employment, affordable housing, and so on. It should also be subject to audit and examination of the People's Congress and supervision by the public. Hebei province will also explore experiments in implementation of participatory budgeting and promote the democratization of budgetary compilation.[9]

The provincial government leaser directly reports to the provincial People's Congress. On September 28, 2010, Chen Min'-er, Executive Vice Governor of Zhejiang province reported on the 20th meeting of the 11th standing committee of the People's Congress on debt management of local government in the province. The report stated that by the end of 2009, debt ratio of provincial government debt in Zhejiang has gone up to 20.15%, 10.15% higher than the warning line. It was the first time for a local provincial government to open the debts of government following disclosure of 2.79 trillion Yuan debts of local governments by the Audit Commission in June 2009. According to the report of *Zhejiang Daily*, the government debts are mainly used for construction of important infrastructure such as railways, airports, and large-scale water conservancy; municipal infrastructure such as water, electricity, gas, affordable housing, mass transit, roads, and bridges; social infrastructure such as education,

---

[9] Hebei will Actively Promote Fiscal Budget Disclosure this Year. *Shijiazhuang City Network*, 2010, 4 (20).

health, and culture; and infrastructure of social services such as rural roads, bridges, and environmental protection.[10]

It is stipulated in the Budget Law that the local budgets at various levels shall be compiled according to the principles of keeping expenditures within the limits of revenues and maintaining a balance between revenues and expenditures, and shall not contain deficit. But in fact a large number of Chinese local governments raise loans even to a degree that are impossible to be completely calculated. Zhejiang provincial government opened information of its debt and requested the national authorities to enact, as soon as possible, uniform management measures on government debt and methods of debt accounting, which represents a responsible attitude.

Information of departmental budgets at the provincial level is requested to be disclosed. Hunan province disclosed budget information of all 124 provincial units starting from 2006. Before the People's Congress meeting and People's Political Consultative conference each year, the deputies to the People's Congress will receive draft budget of various departments and relevant material in advance and two departments are chosen in turn for on-site special examination by some of the deputies. In the meeting of examination of departmental budget review held in 2009, the deputies to the People's Congress from 14 cities and one provincial department were invited to examine budgetary implementation of 2008 and draft budget of 2009 of Department of Water and Land Resources Department. Tan Ke-min, a deputy to the provincial People's Congress said after carefully reading the reports on budget of the two departments that the contents were so comprehensive that they were neither able to tell people where the money was spent nor could help people understand the work of the departments. Zhu Xin-min, Vice Chairman of financial and economic committee of provincial People's Congress, said that such an open and transparent form not only gave the deputies the right to know but also was beneficial to showcase public finance. Chen Shu-hong, deputy director of the standing committee of provincial People's Congress believed that public budgets were to help fiscal budget

[10] Zhejiang Province Announcing that Governments' Debt Ratio in the Province Exceeds Warning Level 10.15%. *21st Century Business Herald*, September 29, 2010. Zhejiang Province For the First Time Disclose Local Governments' Debts. *Southern Weekend*, September 30, 2010.

to achieve the goal of scientific, rational, safe, and efficient. Supervision by the deputies to the People's Congress can cut down randomness of budget, intervention of power on budget, and standardize use of budget funds in various units.[11]

Yang Xiao-Chao, Director of Beijing bureau of finance said when he reported to the standing committee of the municipal People's Congress about financial situation on May 10, 2010 that budget disclosure would be further promoted. Except classified units, all the budgets of government and departments examined and approved by the municipal People's Congress would be disclosed to the civil society. Bureau of finance spokesman Meng Jing-wei then introduced that budget openness of various departments would be more detailed in the next year. The number of departments in Beijing whose budgets were disclosed was 30 in 2009 that later increased to 45 in 2010.[12]

Beijing News reported 10 days later that Beijing began to release budgets online. Beijing education commission, municipal civil affairs bureau, and other departments consequently released their budgets for 2010 in the official websites. Beijing bureau of finance said budgets of 45 departments in Beijing would be released online by the end of May 2010. Starting from 2010, Beijing has published online municipal government budget statements and municipal government budgetary compilation explanation. The released contents only included three simple types: Total budget statements, expenditure budget statements of financial allocation, and budget explanation.

For example, Beijing education commission only released the general figures of total budget report including financial allocations, non-budgetary revenues, business income, and expenditures in education, social security, and employment. At the same time, government expenditures such as reception, trips overseas, and the procurement and maintenance of motor vehicles which are concerned most by the public and basic administrative expenditures of every unit were not mentioned. The released contents are

---

[11] All Provincial Departmental Budgets Disclosed to the People's Congress. *People's Daily*, 2009, 1 (19).

[12] Beijing Municipal Government Departmental Budgets will be Fully Disclosed Next Year. *Beijing News*, 2010, 5 (11).

different from the draft budget and explanations distributed to the deputies during the annual People's Congress session.

Chen Jing-pu, Director of the budget office of the standing committee of the municipal People's Congress said that the contents distributed to the deputies not only included the budget reports but also detailed explanations and even background materials. He said that various departments did not release all these materials mainly for technical reasons. The work process should be done gradually as the disclosure work was time-consuming. Budget disclosure should be detailed and it is a trend. Currently, budgets in Beijing are compiled based on the accounting items of state budgetary revenues and expenditures. The items of revenues and expenditures would be adjusted in favor of more detailed budget accounts and better understanding of the public. Information disclosure in Beijing will further go in detail from current items of the first level to the items of lower level in order to enable the public to know the expenditures of specific projects.[13]

Beijing municipal government requests the departments to open their budgets in given time, which is another big progress. It came after the decision that the central government requires to open government departmental budget, although they are just commitments to the civil society made by the government. As for local governments, the characteristic of their budgets differ from central departments as local financial expenditures of administrative expenses, expenditures concerned with citizens' livelihood, and official consumptions are mainly cared by the civil society. Any disclosure of these expenditures will not only enhance the fiscal performance and authority of the governments but also improve the governments' self-discipline. The details of the departmental revenues and expenditures in Beijing cannot be understood by the public and expenditures of the projects concerned most by the civil society are not mentioned, let alone financial information or material explanations. Budget information of the government departments disclosed online is just to reach the bottom line of information disclosure. To reach the goal of making the public satisfied with disclosure of government budgets, measures

[13] Beijing 45 Departments will Disclose their Budgets Online this Month. *Beijing News*, 2010, 5 (21).

should be taken to have the public understand and be satisfied with information disclosure following online disclosure of budget information.

In 2010, the number of departments submitting detailed departmental budget in Shanghai reached up to 100 from 35 and the budgets of all municipal departments except classified and state secret units were submitted to the People's Congress for examination. Some deputies to the People's Congress pointed it out that more budgets in Shanghai are submitted to them for examinations and supervision and transparency of budget information disclosure is increasing each year, but there is still a gap between the goal of public finance and the requirements of the deputies to the People's Congress. Shanghai municipal finance bureau says that the first step is to further increase the number of municipal departments where budgets are submitted to the municipal People's Congress.

It needs to further detail the draft budget at municipal level and gradually expand the level of fund from category to item level based on original classification of expenditure function. It can be listed by items of class level, make special compilation explanations for the specific contents, and revenues and expenditures listed in the draft. Contents of budget on governmental financial revenues and expenditures will be included in report submitted to the People's Congress. Since the first meeting of 13th Shanghai municipal People's Congress, financial department has begun to assign staff to take part in examination when the delegations are examining the budgets. Budget committee makes a commitment to this practice in the future. Furthermore, the municipal People's Congress will work with relevant departments and some deputies to track the whole process of departmental budgets in real time compilation, implementation. The standing committee of the municipal People's Congress will annually choose one or two key departments to track and supervise the whole process of departmental budget.

On January 4, 2011, Shanghai finance committee and budget work committee of the People's Congress held a meeting for explaining Report on Implementation of Budget of 2010 and Draft Budget for 2011 in Shanghai. The report has greatly improved in comparison with previous years. Budgets of all the municipal departments in Shanghai will be submitted to the Shanghai People's Congress for examination and explanations for compilation of departmental budget drafted by relevant departments will be added in. It means that the management system of Shanghai departmental budget made further improvement. The Report designates a chapter to report on implementation of budgetary resolutions of the People's Congress by relevant departments of government in past year.

Following the Plan for the Implementation of Further Promoting Municipal Budget Information Openness officially promulgated previously, in the departmental budgets submitted to the Municipal People's Congress for examination, some of the departments that are most directly and realistically related to the interests of the public will be chosen for experiments in initiatively disclosing their sums of the departmental budgets of expenditure, basic expenditures, and the sums of expenditure budget of projects to the civil society. According to the Plan, as for improvement of government budgetary system, budgets of state-owned capital management and revenues and expenditures of social insurance funds will be included in submission to the People's Congress based on general budgets of revenues and expenditures and government fund budget.[14]

Shanghai's practice of budget information disclosure in two consecutive years not only makes progress in fulfilling commitments of the government, but also makes a big step in legislation for guaranteeing the system construction of budget information disclosure. This is a good legislative pilot of local governments in advancing financial budget information disclosure step by step and can serve as a model for other provinces. Meanwhile, the system can be constantly improved.

Budget information is disclosed in time for supervision. Viewed from the perspective of budget information disclosure, Guangdong is undoubtedly one of the earliest provinces which disclosed budget information and made various explorations in practice and innovations in institutions. In 2001, in the fourth Meeting of the ninth Guangdong provincial People's Congress seven pilot units submitted their detailed draft budget, marking the end of examination of a mere formality. In 2002, the Guangdong provincial government submitted a draft budget involving 27 departments and

[14]All the Shanghai Municipal Department Budgets will be Submitted to the People's Congress for Examination. *First Financial News*, 2011, 1 (5).

consisting of up to 144 pages. In 2003, the provincial government submitted Report on Budget of Provincial Departments in Guangdong Province with 605 pages, involving the annual budgets of all the 102 provincial government departments with each item clearly listed and detailed.

In 2004, substantial examination supervision of draft budget was started with a budget report. In September 2004, Guangdong Province launched a real-time online financial supervision system, which facilitates the department of finance and economic committee of the Guangdong provincial People's Congress to directly connect with the centralized treasury payment system for real-time online supervision over implementation of provincial budgets. Through the real-time online financial supervision system, the department of finance and economic committee of the People's Congress and deputies could timely retrieve information on every sum of centralized treasury payment in a certain departmental budget, thus enhancing supervision of the People's Congress over implementation of departmental budgets. The system of real-time online financial budgetary supervision is an innovation for strengthening the external supervision and every penny spent by the government can be immediately supervised by the People's Congress.

In recent years, the deputies to the Guangdong provincial People's Congress began to request the government not only to open budget information to the deputies, but also to the whole society. In March 2010, Guangdong provincial government issued Main Points of Administrative Affairs in Guangdong 2010, putting forward to make steady progress in information disclosure of government budgets and final accounts. It is stipulated in the document that information disclosure of budgets and final accounts will be steadily promoted. According to the laws and regulations of the state and related working plans, Guangdong province will actively and steadily push forward budget information disclosure, standardize the contents, methods and scope of information disclosure of the local government, guide and supervise them over timely information disclosure in accordance with the laws. This document serves as a guideline for promoting disclosure of budget information in Guangdong province and implies that Guangdong province will solve the issue of budget information disclosure from the aspect of institution, including standardization of all aspects of budget information disclosure and supervision over implementation of disclosure rather than making some innovations in disclosure of some key parts.

Hubei province is also one of the earliest provinces disclosing budget information. Disclosure is the precondition and means of supervision. To promote scientific decision-making, social supervision, and democratic financing — financial departments of the province put disclosure of government affairs as a compulsory requirement for financial management and made a breakthrough in construction of e-government affairs based on information technology, and public websites. The provincial government remains committed to real, timely, frequent, and complete disclosure. This is done through, improving the media of disclosure, enriching the contents of disclosure, expanding the scope of disclosure of government affairs, ensuring the people, departments and units the rights to information, right to participate, and right to supervise and promote administrative ability in accordance with the laws.

Provincial department of finance regards construction of e-government affairs as the breakthrough of disclosure of financial affairs, constantly making innovations in approaches of disclosure of government affairs. The government actively makes full use of technologies of financial information network to increase transparency of work, expand the channels of public supervision, strengthen supervision, and control of financial behaviors. Critical issues concerning development and reform of public finance and people's interests except those involving state secrets will be disclosed to the civil society in order to reach the goal of establishment of operating system and creation of stable finance.[15]

In 2005, Hubei Province made experiments in disclosure of fiscal and government affairs in 14 cities and districts, which was popularized in March 2006. Information of special fiscal funds and government affairs were gradually disclosed and compilation and implementation of departmental budgets were included in disclosure in 2006.

In 47 disclosed special funds, the funds concerned most by the people and grass-root governments are: funds of two exemptions and one subsidy

[15] Hubei Finance Office Strengthen Network Construction to Promote Government Information Openness. http://xxzx.mof.gov.cn/zhengwuxinxi/jingyanjiaoliu/200812/t20081208_95654.html (Accessed on December 8, 2008).

for poor students and maintenance of dangerous buildings in rural primary and middle schools; funds for rural waterworks, funds for transfer training of rural labor, funds for superior agricultural production, direct food subsidies, seed subsidies, funds for rural comprehensive reform of administration by raising money, land reclamation fees, subsidies to conversion of cropland to forest, living allowances for urban residents, funds for land acquisition and resettlement compensation, and so on. By the end of 2007, provincial financial departments disclosed 54 key special funds involving vital interests of the people, 17.963 billion Yuan in total, involving 3995 person and more than 210,000 items. Various districts actively expand disclosure of 3.2 billion Yuan of special funds online. Budgets of 2783 departments were disclosed with 10.6 billion Yuan involved.[16]

Section 2. Ensuring Citizens' Right to Know on Budget Information

1. Legalization of Citizens' Right to Know on Budget Information

Budget is the central part of interest among various hierarchies in social relationship of the modern society and a hub of distribution of political powers. The budget of a country or a region can make people victims or beneficiaries of government policies. Thus, budget is essentially not only a unilateral matter of the government, but also a matter of all the people. U.S. Supreme Court Justice Marshall once said that the power to tax involves the power to destroy. As the targets are affected directly by the budgets — citizens should pay close attention to movements of the funds and the game between government policies. They should also duly understand whether or not it is implemented in accordance with the commitments made at the meetings of the People's Congress in order to have people's welfare guaranteed. Otherwise, it is difficult to predict whether the government will follow the intention of individual leaders. Else it may go astray from the true demands of the civil society, since the power of allocations on the funds is in the hands of the government. In a sentence,

[16] China Development Research Foundation. *Public Budgets Reader*, Beijing: China Development Press, 2008: 90–91.

budget is not a simple issue involving technologies or tools and it needs people's participation, supervision and evaluation.

Democracy should be concrete and the people should determine their own businesses. Naturally people should know what is going to be decided and what is the premise of decision-making. Budget is the representation of powers and its ultimate target is decision-making for their own affairs by the civil society, namely budgetary democracy, even though the powers are distributed in a complicated way in the process. As for budgetary democracy, either representative democracy or democracy of direct public participation, the main task of budgetary decision-making is disclosure of budget information. The purpose of disclosure to representative agencies is to have budgets examined and supervised by representatives of the people, while the purpose of disclosure to the public is to guarantee citizens right to information, right to participate, and right to supervise.

Chinese President Hu Jin-tao, pointed out that the government should improve the democratic system, enrich the forms of democracy, expand democratic channels, carry out democratic election, guarantee people's right to know, right to participate, right to express, and right to supervise and ensure people to be the masters in accordance with laws. Government should encourage people in democratic decision-making, democratic management, and democratic supervision when he was delivering the report on the 17th CCP National Congress. The speech shows that the government budget information is not only the basic premise of budgetary and political democracy but also protection of citizens' fundamental rights. The reason why right to know is a basic right is that citizens' right to express, right to supervise the government and right to participate in management of state affairs relies upon information. Also implementation of all the fundamental rights will be impossible if there are no basic information. Therefore, government information disclosure is the prerequisite of political democracy and budget information disclosure is one of the main parts of government information disclosure.

Viewed from the legal perspective, China's local budgetary supervision has been gradually improved since its reform and opening up. Majority of the supreme laws such as Constitution and the Organic Law of the People's Congress to the Budget Law, the Audit Law, the Supervision Law, Budget Administrative Regulations, and departmental rules and regulations have gradually standardized provincial budgetary supervision system and developed related regulations of budgetary supervision based on the process of reform of fiscal management system. Especially in recent years when the means of social information has developed fast and public enthusiasm for participating in budgetary supervision has risen — budget information disclosure has become one of the most important works of provincial governments.

The ultimate target of all work of budget information disclosure is to protect citizens' right to know on budget, and thus conduct basic work of protecting the fundamental rights of citizens. Although right to know is not literally expressed in the text of the Constitution, it can be inferred from its articles that it is the precondition of citizens' participation in management of national and social affairs and it is emphasized in the report of the 17th CCP National Congress. As for budgetary supervision, citizens are naturally granted rights to understand basic information of public fiscal revenues and expenditures and they get to learn more about flow of government's public budget funds.

Since the concept of the right to know has been created, its basic contents such as scope, border, body, and ways of exercise should be defined by the laws. Some scholars set up a legal concept that the so-called taxpayer's right to know means the taxpayer is entitled by law to know and gain information from relevant national authorities about laws and regulations on tax, basis of tax collection, procedures of tax collection, use of tax, provision of public production and public services, and the corresponding obligations of relevant national authorities to initiatively disclose and notify.[17] This concept illustrates on the whole legal relationship existing in budget information disclosure and perfectly combines exercise of the citizens' rights with legal relationship between the citizens and the government. Unfortunately the National People's Congress and provincial People's Congress do not pay attention to this issue. Since the right to know on budget information exists as a legal right to information, there are no laws to define all the aspects of this right.

[17] Hua Guo-qing. On Taxpayers' Right to Know and Legal Protection. *Jurist*, 2006, (2): 94.

Budget information disclosure in various provinces is not standardized and the scope, border of the right, and operational procedures of relief are not defined.

People's right to know is the base of a democratic society. Although right to know is not explicitly expressed in the text of the Constitution, realization of all the fundamental rights of citizens relies on the basic requirements of information of the agent — the government. The existence of the state and the government is based on delivery of private property of the civil society and all the funds except the essential part for the government's role of night watchman should be used for development of the civil society in a fair and open way. The reason why the civil society is willing to deliver a great amount of private property is because individuals cannot guarantee their fundamental rights and consequently they must depend on the public powers of a strong government. As a result the government's budget revenue becomes a unique force for protecting the fundamental rights of citizens. Therefore, the budget funds must be used for the purpose of protecting the fundamental rights of citizens and in the way of making people realize the use of public funds based on the precondition of disclosure and transparency of budget.

Citizens entrust the government to perform the basic functions of social management. Nevertheless, the government cannot collect tax or spend public fiscal funds unless they are allowed by the taxpayers. Opinions of civil society on expenditures of public funds are based on information of the funds, and thus forming the concept of citizens' right to know on budget information. Complete disclosure of budget information will not only enable the deputies to the People's Congress to fully perform their functions of examination but also allow the civil society to properly understand information, bring forward claims to the government, and supervise the government for prompt response for the sake of better use of the fiscal funds. Budget openness is the foundation of modern democratic political interaction and is in favor of people's fundamental rights on participation in democratic decision-making, democratic management, and democratic supervision in accordance with the laws. Citizens have the right to fully understand the use of fiscal funds and accordingly the government must take initiatives to disclose all budget information to the civil society.

2. Approaches of Protecting Citizens' Right to Know on Budget Information

Right to know on budget information should be protected by the Constitution and the laws. The National People's Congress should consider adopting the contents of right to know, right to express, right to participate, and right to supervise expressed on 17th Chinese Communist Party (CCP) National Congress in the Constitution and the laws. Current constitution only mentions citizens' obligations to pay taxes but lacks protection of citizens' financial rights. This is unfavorable to enacting of lower laws to protect citizens' right to know. In this case, various provinces can develop budget information disclosure system in regulations of budgetary supervision on legal basis.

Currently, China has no uniform Law of Financial Supervision for standardizing budgetary supervision. The relevant laws and regulations are scattered in all levels. The purpose and guideline may not be completely unified and there are no specific local regulations of budget information disclosure. It's necessary to combine provincial regulations of budgetary supervision with regulations of fiscal information disclosure; at the same time have the regulations of information disclosure by the State Council upgraded to laws formulated by the National People's Congress. The laws, regulations, and local rules of government information disclosure of the state and the provincial regulations should reflect uniform guideline. The present practice that the provinces make their own regulations of budget openness as required by the national ministry of finance should be changed and it is necessary to provide the government information disclosure system with protection from the level of law. The contents of the related laws should also be clear and relief measures should be definite.

In the specific procedure of making laws of budget information disclosure, the first thing that should be paid attention to is the principles in disclosure. Current situation of budget information disclosure appears to be despondent, partially because the government departments have no clear principles in disclosure. The laws and regulations on budget information disclosure must highlight the principle of disclosure. At the same time, the procedures of realizing the rights and performance of the duties of related authorities must be standardized. The scope of budget information and the extent of disclosure should be clearly defined. The channels and manners of disclosure should be regulated and all the disclosed budget information must be in line with generally accepted standards of accounting and statistics in order to facilitate the public and the People's Congress to look up, compare, and analyze.

Budget information disclosure is an obligation of the governments and relevant measures of relief should be available to protect citizens' right to know upon any violation by the governments. Legal protection of the right to know on budget information disclosure must be considered in mechanism for the protection of the Constitution, constitutional laws and regulations and it should resort to administrative or even constitutional proceedings if necessary. Therefore, it needs to enact provisions of relief for appeal and establish judicial channels of remedies through lawsuit system and change the current situation with few relief measures.

Supervision does not completely rely on representative agencies as they are only representatives of the public whose opinions cannot be fully considered by the representative agencies. Without supervision of the public, the powers of government public expenditures sometimes can be controlled by a few people whose decisions often have the taxpayers suffer immense losses. Citizens do not have enough sense of supervision and their initiative for budgetary supervision is insufficient. Highly developed information technology in civil society should have been tools of public opinions for budgetary supervision. Defects in the governments' public finance management can be improved after exposure in the public media. All opinions from social professional agencies, experts, scholars, and citizens should be considered in the decision-making system on the governments' major public expenditures plan or significant projects and their wisdom should be utilized to assist the People's Congress to make their contribution in budgetary supervision.

Chapter 6

The Third Part of System Improvement: Improvement of Budgetary Supervision Procedure

Supervision of the People's Congress over the government budget is involved in the whole budgetary process. This includes approval of the draft budget, supervision over the process of budgetary implementation, approval of budgetary adjustment, and audit of the budgetary implementation situation. It also involves collection and feedback of the public opinions. The most serious problem of budgetary supervision of the provincial People's Congress in China is its failure in substantive results, as the laws and regulations passed by both the national and the provincial People's Congress only define the contents of budgetary supervision rather than providing practical supervision measures. This makes it difficult for the People's Congress to exercise substantive supervision over the fiscal revenues and expenditures of the government in accordance with corresponding legal provisions. Therefore, it needs to strengthen legal construction of the People's Congress in decision-making of budgetary compilation and implementation, regulating the budgetary powers of the government, and solving the problem in practice that budgetary supervision power of the People's Congress is weak or even empty.

Section 1. Proposal for Strengthening Supervision System in the Whole Process

1. To Strengthen Legislative for Involvement of the People's Congress in Budgetary Process

As the People's Congress supervision over budgetary implementation is essentially a legal supervision and thus it is necessary to improve the legal system of budgetary supervision. If the Constitution and the local laws and regulations do not grant expressly supervision powers over budgetary implementation to the provincial People's Congress or do not provide practical measures, then the People's Congress supervision over budgetary implementation can only be regarded as accepting afterwards rather than correcting or punishing functions in the process, as the government departments and their officials do not have real accountability.

At present, in laws ranging from the Supervision Law to the Budget Law and the Audit Law, terms for budgetary supervision of the People's Congress are too general in principle and the local laws and regulations in various provinces are just to quote and explain the principles and definitions. There are no systematic, comprehensive, and operational regulations so that even though the provincial People's Congress is aware of its role in routine supervision, its deep participation in supervision is not supported by related legal provisions.

In the most important programs of budgetary supervision, the People's Congress supervision is facing two immense obstacles: one is no power of draft budget amendment, and the other is no active participation in supervision over the process of budgetary implementation. Both obstacles can only be changed by legislature. The power of budget amendment must be granted through revising the Budget Law, otherwise the current ways through which votes in which the budgets are passed or rejected as a whole cannot allow the deputies to the People's Congress to really exercise the power of amending or vetoing the draft budget.

Although the Budget Law and Supervision Law have defined the contents and scope of the supervision of the standing committee of the People's Congress in the course of budgetary implementation, there are no legal regulations for operational measures and it is difficult for the People's Congress to take the initiatives to take part in supervision over the process of budgetary implementation or even more difficult to take coercive measures against the government's violations in budgets. Therefore, the local regulations or normative documents about budgetary supervision passed by the People's Congress in various provinces must define the scope, content, and procedures of budgetary supervision of the People's Congress. It should also provide strict operational regulations on budgetary supervision.

Enhancing participation of the People's Congress in examination of the budget should be the focal point of strengthening legislation. Provincial People's Congress should consider to push the representative of the communities to join in the budgetary examination group in order to ensure comprehensiveness of the budget allocation, legally protect the budgetary examination powers of the group, and make regulations on intensifying the group's coordination with the government departments, especially the audit department. There should be a rule to figure out statutory reports of examination and survey before the People's Congress session in order to be discussed in meetings of the deputies as important basis of budgetary supervision.

Improvement of the budgetary organization of the People's Congress is also an emphasis of supervisory legislation for institutional protection. It needs to establish an independent budgetary supervision department within the People's Congress with experts of professional knowledge, who will improve the system of supervision institutions and supporting organizations. It also needs to further ensure that the deputies have enough time to fulfill their duties and strengthen support organization and system that can assist the deputies in their work.[1] The powers of investigation into specific issues can only be truly exercised by the People's Congress and its standing committee through such endeavor.

2. To Improve the Procedures of Supervision Over Performance in Budgetary Process

In terms of supervisory procedures, the role of budgetary supervision of the People's Congress in the early stage is mainly to participate in

[1] Zou Ping-xue. On Professional Deputies to the People's Congress. *Institutional Structure of Democracy in China*, Shanghai: Shanghai People's Publishing House, 2008: 75.

budgetary compilation and amendment. But it should make reasonable plans for the revenues and expenditures in advance because the implementation of the plan, especially the effectiveness and efficiency of the financial budget expenditures for public administration can only be known after the implementation. The People's Congress can only really supervise the whole budgetary process of the government following reasonable evaluation of the performance of budgetary implementation.

It will have positive impact on building responsible governments and providing more reliable reference for budgetary supervision in the future. Hence, the supervision laws and regulations should provide statutory procedures through which the People's Congress can evaluate the budgetary performance. Also, if the People's Congress thinks it is necessary to know the effectiveness of the financial budget in the course of budgetary implementation at any moment, there should be regulations for how to start the statutory evaluation procedures.

Guangdong bureau of finance issued Experiment Scheme of Evaluation of Performance of Financial Expenditures in Guangdong in 2004, to start evaluating the performance of financial expenditures. The objective of this move is to strengthen the management of financial expenditures, to establish a scientific–standardized and efficient allocation and management system of financial resources, and gradually change the present situation of financial management to improve efficiency of the provincial financial resources and further promote economic development and fight against corruption.

Article 5 provides that performance of provincial items of expenditures over 5 million Yuan are to be evaluated for experimentation. The last paragraph of Article 4 provides that in evaluating performance, when necessary, special committee of the People's Congress, the deputies, and CPPCC members can be invited to attend. Consequently, the People's Congress of Guangdong Province took the opportunity to actively exercise supervision over the financial expenditure performance and actively participated in supervision over performance of the expenditures. The provincial People's Congress in 2005 organized supervision over the performance of the fiscal funds for several times, examined use of the funds allocated for reconstruction of primary schools in the remote and old areas, assessed the use of the funds of financial discount loans for college infrastructure, and evaluated performance of research activities.[2]

In 2009, the standing committee of Beijing People's Congress for the first time regarded supervision over the performance of fiscal funds as an important part to improve and strengthen the budgetary supervision of the People's Congress and urged the municipal government to strengthen the process through performance audit, promoting a reasonable budgetary compilation and rational use of the funds. In an interview, Du De-yin, the director of the standing committee of the Beijing People's Congress pointed out that the so-called performance supervision is a better combination of supervision over budgetary compilation, adjustment and implementation with supervision over performance of the use of the budget funds. In short, it is to prevent certain departments, to a certain extent, from easily obtaining money and freely spending it.[3]

Audit department can follow requirements of the standing committee of the People's Congress to investigate the use of financial funds of departments, can accurately find idle funds and assets and low efficiency of the use, and can recommend the government to consider evaluation of the performance to assess various departments. For example, in the funds invested in rural compulsory education, some schools that are small in size and only have tens of students applied appropriation based upon 500 students. Chen Jing-pu, Director of the budget office of the standing committee of the municipal People's Congress said that authenticity, legitimacy of the projects are all right — there is no misappropriation and embezzlement, but the efficiency is not high and from an economic point of view, effectiveness is not maximized. The greatest advantage of such supervision is to drive the various departments in budgetary compilation to pay more attention to the detail and actual efficiency in the use, finally achieving the goal of making the whole financial budget more reasonable.

---

[2] China Development Research Foundation. *Public Budgets Reading*, Beijing: China Development Press, 2008: 181.

[3] Financial and Economic Committee of Beijing People's Congress Review the Report of the Government on Performance of the Spendings for the First Time. *Beijing News*, 2010, 1 (21).

This can only solve the initial problem, which defines the contents of the performance to be supervised, but there is no strict regulations on the approaches and procedures of supervision over the performance. It needs to define in the provincial regulations on budgetary supervision — the procedures, inquiry and accountability mechanisms for the People's Congress to evaluate the budgetary performance and the scope of statutory materials that should be correspondingly provided by the government departments.

3. To Promote the System of Civil Participation and Supervision

The citizens who are the most direct participators in the process of the government budgetary implementation certainly will be eligible to participate in supervision over the budgetary implementation. Currently in China the channels to participate in supervision is supervision of public opinions through the media, which however, has no statutory effect. In general, the channels to relieve the citizens' rights to participate in the budgetary supervision are litigation and prosecution. The strictest supervision of the citizens should be supervision of litigation; although there is no precedent in the system this sort of supervision must be explored.

The resident litigation, a taxpayer lawsuit originating from the U.S. case law in the post-war democratic construction, has become a unique system of supervision over local budgetary implementation in Japan. In 1995, almost all states in the U.S. admitted that the communities of taxpayers in the counties, cities and towns of the state can perform taxpayer proceedings, or even 34 states explicitly recognized the state taxpayer litigation and only two states held a negative position in state taxpayer litigation. Chapter 9 of Local Rule Act in Japan designates ten sections discussing inspection request and litigation of the residents with the direct objective of preventing and correcting illegal or improper financial acts of the staff of local public agencies, and the system provides the residents with the means to participate in local politics and local administration, protects local interests, supervises, and legally audits the financial operations of the local public agencies.

Resident litigation in Japan believes in public proceedings by the citizens, thereby, enabling the individuals to play an effective role in the implementation of the laws. In 1990s, several resident litigations were brought aiming at social expenditures and entertainment expenses of the government departments. For instance, in 1999 Akita district, the plaintiff requested the court to judge that 6 officials pay off the 2,091,245 Yen food expenses which was illegally spent. The court finally recognized the plaintiff's request to sentence the defendant to pay the sum of money and interest and the burden of litigation costs.[4]

However, in China there is no any detailed operational regulation on such a system. As abstract administrative act cannot bring an administrative lawsuit, it is difficult to distinguish the behavior of public budget of the government between the specific administrative acts or abstract administrative acts. But local financial budget funds directly provide the society with public goods, most in the public domain, which directly impact the daily life of the citizens. Nevertheless, it should legally protect the citizens' power of participation in supervision and establish the channels allowing the citizens to request the People's Congress to launch a special investigation into budgetary behaviors of the government.

The Constitution provides that citizens of the People's Republic of China the right to criticize and make suggestions regarding any state organ or functionary. Citizens have the right to make complaints or charges against relevant state organs, or expose any state organ or functionary for violation of the law or dereliction of duty. Article 39 of Supervision Law provides that the standing committee of the People's Congress needs to make a resolution or decision on the matter within its own jurisdiction. When it is unclear about the relevant important facts, the People's Congress can organize an investigation committee for the specific issues.

Protecting citizens' right of prosecution in the course of budgetary implementation means ensuring citizens' participation in budgetary supervision. For instance, in the example illustrated in Chapter 3 of this book, Guangdong Province invested tens of millions of Yuan of provincial financial budget in the official kindergartens in seven consecutive years. The

---

[4]Yan Hai. Multiple Supervision over the Implementation of the Budget in Japan Based on Constitutional System. *Jiangsu Social Sciences*, 2010, (2): 146.

public believed that some of the governmental officials were making profits with the money of the taxpayers and their acts infringed the rights of education of their children. It also violated the principles of equity in education and socialization of logistics, and were signs of typical unfair behaviors of the government. The citizens are very sensitive to the effects of input and output of public funds, from the perspective of the effective supervision of the budget funds. There is a need to establish a system allowing the citizens to prosecute the case of using financial budget funds that they believe directly affects their livelihood and request the People's Congress to make investigation.

To improve the system of citizens' participation in budgetary supervision is one of the important contents of improving the People's Congress budgetary supervision. Since China has not yet established a system of citizen's budgetary proceedings, therefore, as legislative body and representative agency the People's Congress should effectively supervise financial budget behaviors of the government with reasonable public powers through the legal system. In the meantime citizens should participate in the course of budgetary supervision, especially when citizens feel that the government's budgetary allocation or other specific financial administrative acts infringe their fundamental rights. With consideration of particularity of the budgetary supervision and statutory functions and powers of the People's Congress, it needs to design a reasonable system to allow citizens to request the People's Congress to make special budget investigation and urge the government to eventually take up the responsibility.

Section 2. Improvement of the Supervision Procedure in the Stage of Budgetary Compilation

1. Strengthen the Supervision in Making Decision in Budget at the Provincial Level

Political importance of the budgetary process can be shown in many ways. Firstly, it affects distribution of powers between the government's administrative and legislative agencies as well as the government and the public (individuals and organized interest groups).[5] The reason why the government does not want the People's Congress to intervene too much in financial budget affairs is that in China's social development there is always government-centered concept, that is to say, the government always feels that they raise the money by themselves and make development plans by themselves, and consequently assessment should also be done by themselves. On specific issues such as submission of the budget proposals, even though according to the related laws and regulations such as the Budget Law, the government should submit its budget report to the People's Congress levels for examination one month before the meetings. In fact the laws or regulations neither regulate the responsibility of failure in submitting on time nor define what specific items to be submitted. The People's Congress has very little time to examine the budgets and the contents submitted are not detailed enough, making it difficult for the financial and economic committee of the provincial People's Congress and the working committee of the standing committee to comprehensively evaluate the draft budget, and eventual approval will inevitably become a mere formality.

Transition from high centralization to fragmented decentralization of Chinese provincial budget decision-making system causes great trouble to budgetary supervision of the People's Congress. As a result, a core budget institution never forms and expenditure decentralization becomes too serious. Professor Ma Jun and Professor Hou Yi-lin came to a conclusion after empirical studies of the provincial budgetary system in China that the fragmentation tendency of the budgetary power structure appears at the high level of provincial politics. In provincial politics, the powers of the provincial Party secretary and the governor must be to a certain degree decentralized or shared by the vice governors and other members of the provincial standing committee.

According to the logic of division of the functions, each vice governor is in charge of a few areas of policy; each member of the standing committee is in charge of some fields, sometimes the Party affairs and sometimes areas of policy of the government. In provincial politics,

[5] Ellen Rubin. *Public Budget Politics: Revenues and Expenditure, Debts and Balance*, Beijing: China Renmin University Press, 2001: 88.

usually there are nearly 20 such leaders. The areas of policy that these leaders are in charge of are in fact, their territories of policy. In general, all the leaders have almost exclusive powers in their own territories. Moreover, each leader is supported by some officials. Although, the Constitution passed in 1982 and the Budget Law passed in 1994 grant the People's Congress power to examine, approve, and supervise budgets of the government — up to the recent reform of departmental budget the People's Congress have not participated in the budgets.

As the People's Congress cannot really exercise the budgetary powers in the process of budgetary compilation, the budgetary powers are replaced by the administrative budgetary system mainly consisting of the Party committee and the government. However, in a fragmented authoritarian regime, the power structure within the administrative budgetary system is fragmented and in such a situation, China's budgetary system will not be able to establish a centralized core budget institution to unify the allocation of funds and have the financial allocation of powers that are originally controlled by the Party committee and the planning commission fragmented to various departments.[6] Such a fragmented budget decision-making system makes it very difficult to establish a central budget decision-making department and thus increases the cost and difficulty of budgetary supervision of the provincial People's Congress.

According to audit results, in many years in provincial finance in China, enormous non-budgetary funds exist and the scope and power of the various territories of policy are growing, thereby, increasing the difficulty of supervision. On the one hand, as the policy-making power is fragmented — all the leaders have a policy-making power and they will have corresponding power of expenditures. Of course, to what extent can the leaders affect the financial allocation depends on the relative distribution of the powers between the governors and other leaders, in particular, on their political support in the Party and their respective political network. If the governor is relatively weak, other leaders can affect more on the financial distribution.

[6] Ma Jun, Hou Yi-lin. Informal System of Provincial Budgets in China: A Theory Framework of Transaction Cost. *Economic Research*, 2004, (10): 16.

On the other hand, the fragmented and out-of-date formal budgetary system cannot provide a relatively rational budget structure, procedures and rules for examination. It gives opportunities for these politicians to informally penetrate into the formal budget structure, procedures and rules.[7] In the light of the reality of politics of provincial budget, it needs to make exploration in improving the supervision mode of the provincial People's Congress for legal scholarship.

At present, as the local government bears a lot of investment mandate, the provincial People's Congress can strengthen the supervision over areas of government investment and major expenditures. After empirical researches in a province, some scholars believe that, firstly, the People's Congress should veto expenditure items to show its capacities in changing the budgets. Vetoing items of expenditures listed in the draft budget is an important indicator of the influence of the People's Congress in the budget process.[8] At the provincial level, allocation of investment funds is relatively dispersed, and to a certain extent investment funds are controlled by the government departments.

The governments at the county or municipal levels and their departments can also apply appropriation from the provincial departments for their projects and investment and most of these funds are allocated to the county or municipal departments by the provincial departments in accordance with complicated relationship among them. This means that the county or municipal financial departments or planning departments cannot manage these funds at all or not obtain any information about them. What is more, local governments below the provincial level can get subsidies or financial appropriation not only from the central government but also the provincial financial departments or planning departments. This makes it more difficult to regulate investment management of the governments below the provincial levels.[9] Provincial People's Congress should define in detail the terms of supervision over the key expenditures and

---

[7] Ma Jun, Hou Yi-lin. Informal System of Provincial Budgets in China: A Theory Framework of Transaction Cost. *Economic Research*, 2004, (10): 17.

[8] Lin Mu-hua. Reshape Budgetary Powers of the People's Congress: Based on Surveys in a Province. *Public Administration Review*, 2008, (4): 165.

[9] Ma Jun, Zhou Yan. On Decision-making System of Chinese Provincial Government Investment: A Case Study. *Public Management Research*, 2008, (4): 31.

make them operational in accordance with the Supervision Law and the regulations on budgetary supervision in various provinces.

As to the government investment projects, the feasibility report should be reviewed from the very beginning and projects of major construction needs rigid examination. And in the course of implementation it needs continuous tracking and supervision, frequently reviewing audit reports and reports of other departments on the implementation of the projects. It needs to hold several discussions and consultation with the government in order to help make rational decisions. In some areas there have been regulations that large-scale projects in which investment is beyond a given amount must be submitted to the People's Congress for examination; some local People's Congress has made regulations that large-scale projects must be voted in advance. The People's Congress should make full use of the professional role of the audit departments and strengthen supervision over investment projects, state-owned assets management and public funds of the government. As to major expenditures the budget should be detailed in items of amount from current items of class.

2. Strengthen the Unification of the Budgetary Powers

Professor Wang Shao-guang from the Chinese University of Hong Kong believes that in China there are some problems not only in budgetary supervision but also in financial unification aspects. As to the financial unification, the most serious problem of China's budgetary system is lack of complete and unified public budgets covering all revenues and expenditures of the government. In terms of budgetary supervision, compilation of detailed functional budgets of the government and departmental budgets can greatly facilitate the deputies to the People's Congress to make budget examination and supervision. Obviously, in financial unification and budgetary supervision, China still has a long way to go.

Since financial unification is as important as budgetary supervision, it seems that interactive improvement of both aspects should become the mode through which China intends to carry out state budget.[10] If sources of financial income of the Chinese grass-roots governments are not

[10] Wang Shao-guang. From Tax Country to Budget Country. *Dushu*, 2007, (10): 12–13.

effectively regulated, government expenditures lack openness and transparency and budgetary supervision is not operational, the government size will keep expanding and the government debts will keep increasing, which will lead to more corruption out of control and more dangerous risks in fiscal decentralization between Chinese central and local governments in the process of economic development.

Decentralization of government budget will make it more difficult for the representative agencies to supervise and control the budget. Current provincial cases of budget in China are very similar to those of the U.S. in the Progressive Era. The U.S. has smoothly solved the problems of the parliamentary budgetary supervision by budget reform from the local urban governments to congressional departments and at the same time allowed the government to maintain a strong budget leadership, and a system of good communications and consultations with the Congress.

The U.S. is the country with best budgetary supervision announced by OECD. Its experience of transition from a tax nation to a budget nation in the Progressive Era reflects the historical process of formation of the public supervision over the government behaviors. Of course, although the U.S. and China differ in its administrative system and state budgets in the U.S. are different from the provincial budgets in China, the concept of American budgetary reform from national budget to municipal budget is helpful for China.

The system before the Budget and Accounting Bill passed in 1921 allowed administrative agencies to directly apply financial grants from a congressional committee and they were not subject to control of the president and even did not require to follow policy guidelines. Powers of financial allocation controlled directly by the Congress create a system in which the duties of supervision cannot really be fulfilled and the Congress will be unable to supervise and control spending of the administrative agencies once the funds are allocated in package. In such a circumstance, the Congress only has the power of purse in concept without essential powers of controlling the purse on behalf of the people.

In the U.S. previously there were no budgets in the modern sense. Each department of the government looked for funds and controlled the expenditures. The government at a certain level did not have detailed and unified budgets so that the people and the Congress could not effectively supervise the government and its departments, leaving countless opportunities for corruption. Until the early 20th century in the U.S. the so-called budgets were just a bunch of disorganized reported bill after use. The financial allocation to a department of the government was just an amount, with no classification of expenditures or specific items, let alone completeness.

In this case, although the U.S. was known for its democracy — the public was in fact unable to effectively supervise the government behaviors. As the result, corruption kept growing.[11] In the Progressive Era, the U.S. government's fiscal revenues and expenditures were quite different from current situation. The vast majority of expenditures occurred in the local governments, municipal council, and various independent committees shared the powers of financial allocation. The various departments of the government independently seek funds from the municipal council and its committees. This decentralized system led rampant corruption. The U.S. local government was generally believed to be extremely corrupt back then. Expenditures of urban maintenance construction were not recorded and the municipal government had no records of public property and public assets which were frequently lost. Bribery and corruption were quite serious in land lease, public services, public project, and government procurement. The expenditures were quite confusing. In US$140 million of total financial allocation of New York City in 1908, US$8 million were used to repay the special tax bonds, which in fact was used to make up the overrun expenditures of the previous year.[12]

Public budget reform initiatives involve the budgetary system adjustments from local to federal government. American reformers then believed that the Congress had no enthusiasm to control spending of the government and was only interested in spending money on its own supporters. Only the head of the executive considered the overall interests of the area. They believed that the powers were too dispersed and supervision was impossible. The split funding system of the Congress itself had several major defects. Firstly, the public could not participate in supervision,

[11] Wang Shao-guang. *Enlightenment of the U.S. Progressive Era*, Beijing: China Financial and Economic Publishing House, 2002, (6): 3.

[12] Wang Shao-guang. From Tax Country to Budget Country. *Dushu*, 2007, (10): 8.

resulting in waste of public funds; secondly, financial appropriation would increase when appropriation bills were repeatedly discussed in the Senate and the House of Representatives; and thirdly, within the Congress some committees complained that appropriations committee of the House of Representatives had excessive control over other committees.[13] The budget reformers opposed this fragmented budget process as no one paid attention to the total expenditures in this budgetary process.[14]

In the late 19th century, the Congress began to weaken the powers of the appropriations committee. In the early 20th century, in American society two concepts of the public budget was formed namely, the executive-led budget and legislative-led budget. The mainstream view in America then was that regardless of any change in the future, the administrative agencies would play an important role in the budgetary compilation and implementation.[15]

Budgetary reform in the U.S. started from the local government, to be more exact, from New York. The reform of municipal government that started in New York and widely promoted to other cities throughout the country was focused on the system and ways of operation of the government to improve the efficiency of government management. It consisted of reform of government accounting and budget and civil service reform. The focal point was the reform of government accounting with strengthening accounting controls and accurately reflecting the real government financial status; establishing administrative budgetary system to clearly define financial responsibility and designing comprehensive, and detailed budget items, which not only fully reflected the budget activities of the government and allowed the departments to be responsible for the government heads within the government but also enabled them to be responsible for the Congress as well as the citizens.[16]

---

[13] Aaron Wildavsky, Naomi Caiden. *The New Politics of the Budgetary Process*, Beijing: Peking University Press, 2009: 31–32.

[14] Aaron Wildavsky, Naomi Caiden. *The New Politics of the Budgetary Process*, Beijing: Peking University Press, 2009: 34.

[15] A.E. Buck. The Development of the Budget Idea in the United States. *The Annals of the American Academy of Political and Social Science*, 1924, (113): 32–33.

[16] Ma Jun. Economic and Social Changes and Transformation of Governance: Reform of the U.S. Progressive Era. *Public Management Research*, 2008, (6): 29.

For China, the provincial budgetary powers are decentralized due to internal decentralization of the executive powers and provincial budgetary powers need to be controlled by the government and the overall budget resources allocation should be controlled by the governor. The expenditure of the New York City in 1898 was five times of that of New York State and one-seventh more than that of the federal government. In the early 20th century, the New York City was the largest single organization of public finance in the U.S. Model of corporate governance of the municipal government needed openness and transparency of financial information. The reformers adopted corporate accounting techniques in analysis and management of the municipal finance.

Moreover, the accounting system was helpful for citizens' political participation and the government budget information supplied by the accounting records could better guide public participation in political affairs in order to control their government. At the same time the accounting system put forward higher requirements for the administrative departments in transparency of implementation of the plans and planning ability, requiring a centralized and unified power to co-ordinate, which was helpful for the administrative departments headed by the president to strengthen its own position in the budgetary compilation and executive powers.

Budget becomes the basis of certain political allocation of responsibilities by giving the legislature and citizens powers to have the executive departments and their officials responsible for their actions. The budgetary system is a means of improving representative democracy. Within the government, there is an urgent need to define precisely the responsibilities and results of allocation of the departments. As a means budget can break these trivial powers and provide standard information to form a centered power in those departments which powers can be integrated and coordinated. In order to fight against corruption, budget can formalize the boundaries of the public and the private sectors and to improve efficiency budget can get rid of the boundaries to force different departments under the centralized budgetary supervision.[17] Therefore, under the concept of

---

[17] Jonathan Kahn. *Budgeting Democracy — National Building and Citizenship in America (1890–1928)*, Shanghai: Shanghai People's Publishing House, 2008, (8): 59–60.

the public budgetary adjustment, the budgetary power is closely related to changes of government functions and also related to interests of the nation and people.

The administrative power reform in the Progressive Era suggested that a chief executive (President), who was clearly exposed under the supervision of the public at the top of a pyramid of the bureaucratic power could make the government more efficient and responsible, and, under this concept, the Congress gradually became aware that it was necessary and safe to grant the President the power of controlling the executive departments. Scientific and rational budgetary system would become the pivot of the Congress to supervise the President over exercising the powers commissioned by the Congress. Similarly, this concept was recognized by the public and major political figures.

As a part of the political system reform, the necessary basis of budgetary reform had been quite solid. The ideal model should be that the Congress becomes the representative of the people as a whole while the President becomes the representative of the government as a whole. The work the Congress should better engage in how to design a good system to supervise and control the budgetary behaviors of the President on behalf of the government. In terms of specific ways of supervision, the 1921 budget and accounting bill set up the general accounting office that was independent from the administrative departments to assist the Congress in strengthening powers of the government financial supervision. The chief of the general accounting office was nominated and approved by the Senate.

Division in the budgetary powers between the President and the Congress enabled them perform their duties in a better way, in order to achieve the true status and functions in the political system.[18] The Congress could effectively supervise the President over exercising budgetary powers and also required the President to strengthen efforts to control the entire administrative system. If the President was not so strong that could control various departments of the government, there would be no

[18] W.F. Willoughby. *The Budget as an Instrument of Political Reform*. Proceedings of the Academy of the Political Science in the City of New York, *National Conference on War Economy*, 1918, (8): 59.

basis of operation for responsible government.[19] Meanwhile, when the President strengthened unification of leadership of the overall administrative departments, for the people the government would become more transparent, efficient and controllable through the budget. Such an organizational configuration can be referred for the Chinese provincial People's Congress participation in budgetary compilation as the People's Congress can directly understand the government's budgetary compilation with the support of independent organizations and promptly propose amendments to the draft budget.

Budgetary reform had great impacts on development of the political system in the U.S. after the Progressive Era. Corruption existing in the American society was effectively controlled for the first time, thus greatly enhancing the people's trust on the government in general, and at the same time the government's administrative powers were more centralized, unified, efficient, honest and clean. The public budget reform turned the government into a responsible one on behalf of the interests of the people and fundamentally reshaped the governance image of the government at various levels.

Of course, from another angle, various problems and contradictions existing in the American society in the Progressive Era were not originated from the Congress' control of the powers of financial expenditures as even in the era when the powers of financial allocation were held by of the Congress, the government still had administrative powers. The fundamental reason actually was that the Congress could not effectively supervise the government's financial status through a sound supervision mechanism. Congress was beginning to understand that clear definition of the powers and duties was the most important prerequisite for supervision and control and only when the government submitted detailed budget plans, the powers of final approval and supervision of the Congress was well-founded and the following audit system could make sense. The greatest achievement of the public budget reform with strengthening budgetary powers at the core by the President in the Progressive Era was that

[19] Jonathan Kahn. *Budgeting Democracy: National Building and Citizenship in America (1890–1928)*, Shanghai: Shanghai People's Publishing House, 2008, (8): 180.

administrative act got a standard and normal development, building up a sound supervision system.

3. Standardization and Externalization of Procedural Design in the Stage of Budgetary Compilation

Budget behavior is a product of government administrative management and budgetary democracy. It largely depends on the improvement of the government budgetary management systems. Besides, the modern budgetary system is so complicated that clarity of the government budgetary system will directly affect quality of the supervision of the representative agencies and civil society over the public budget. Chinese provincial policy-making system is a fragmented authoritarian system and there are various informal systems in China's provincial budgets, which have a decisive influence on the financial allocation. Although currently in China, the departmental budgetary reform emphasizes budgetary compilation with the zero-based budget, political factors severely restrict the zero-based budget reform in the provincial budgets.

In addition, during the budgetary reform there is no corresponding reform of policy-making system as well as intergovernmental relations in China. In the local budgets, the policy process and the budgetary process are seriously separated.[20] The public budget reform in China should start from a technical issue such as establishing budget accounts (each account lists amount of the funds; the deadline of using the funds; funds allocated to which departments and subordinate agencies of the government, and to be used for the cost of which financial projects and activities) to externalize the budget and promote the budgetary supervision of the whole society with openness and transparency of the budget.

Technical reform will lead to reform at the political level. It is a basic requirement of a modern democratic government to have its budgets entirely in the control of public opinions. It needs to establish a budgetary system of democratic examination based on examination and approval of

[20] Ma Jun, Zhao Zao-zao. Options of the Goals of Budget Reform in China. *Journal of Social Science of Hunan Normal University*, 2005, (5): 40.

the People's Congress and public participation.[21] Therefore, in order to meet the requirements of budgetary democracy in constitutionalism, the government public budget reform should move forward rule of law, democratization and rationalization.

If budgetary acts of the government are discussed with constitutionalism viewpoints, the focal point is not procedural problems between the government departments but the relationship between administrative control and legislative control of budget, namely the relationship between the government and the People's Congress. As local governments have great powers to control budgetary funds and the budgetary system is dominated by the administrative departments — it needs to be changed by a reform of government budgetary management system with the focus of supervision and control of the People's Congress in order to establish a unified fiscal target and force the executive departments to allocate and use all the financial resources under strict budgetary constraints, having all the expenditures of administrative management come from budgetary funds.

As the first local regulation on non-tax revenue management in China, there are some provisions that are still unclear in Regulation on Non-tax Revenue Management of Hunan Province. Articles 18 and 20 of the regulation provides that non-tax revenue is included in consolidated financial management in following ways: (1) administrative fees and charges, income of confiscation, income of the state-owned assets, revenues of the state-owned resources to be managed as general budget; (2) government fund (additional) to be managed as fund budget; (3) fees and other non-tax revenue to be managed as general budget or financial special account in accordance with the relevant provisions of the State. The people's government at all levels should reasonably arrange and use non-tax revenues and the funds of special purpose shall be used for the purposes as expected.

With the legal, political and economic development in China, budgetary compilation, examination, implementation, and supervision are ruled by law, however, as the powers of the People's Congress are weak the budgetary examination and approval are just procedural and the People's

---

[21] Cai Ding-jian. Approaches and Technologies of the Reform of Public Budget. *Chinese Reform*, 2007, (6): 25–26.

Congress cannot effectively exercise budgetary compilation powers, leading most of the reviews not substantive, which needs improvement urgently. Secondly, as the People's Congress is responsible for all citizens, it should provide the public with all budget information from compilation to implementation that is not confidential. However, as the budget information is not disclosed in time, transparency is poor and it is difficult to examine public responsibility is not sufficiently implemented and the public do not pay much attention to the budget. In this way, the political control of the government budget lacks support among the masses and it is difficult to realize democratic financial management.[22]

Government budgetary compilation is not promptly submitted for supervision in China and it operates without supervision at the beginning of implementation. It is necessary to reform the time and procedure arrangements of the budgetary compilation and submission for examination, approval, discussion, negotiation, and hearing. Detailed contents and procedures of the budgetary compilation will facilitate the budgetary supervision of the People's Congress. The government should regulate the scope and procedures of submitting the budgets to the People's Congress for supervision so that it can effectively participate with the public in the process of budgetary supervision.

On the second meeting of the tenth People's Congress of Guangdong Province on February 10, 2004, Provincial Departmental Budget Tables in 2004 (also known as budgetary manual) which has 504 pages, including 115 provincial departments was given to the representatives attending the meeting. In the budget reports, each departmental draft budget is supplied with texts of explanations, clarifying the department's general information, allocation of personnel, tasks in the new fiscal year and explanations for the revenues and expenditures, and some significant items with descriptions in brief. In order to assist the delegates to examine the draft budget, the general assembly for the first time established a planned budget group that specifically provide services related to the budgetary examination for the representatives and give advice upon request. It also

[22] Wen Bing-xun. Administrative Control, Political Control and Public Budget: On the Public Budget Reform in China. *Journal of Social Science of Hunan Normal University*, 2007, (3): 38.

sets up computer systems for the representative for searches. In addition, for the first time it held a meeting of the draft budget forum for widely collecting opinions of the representatives to enhance effectiveness of examination. The series of initiatives stimulated the unprecedented enthusiasm of the majority of the representatives and almost all of the representatives praised that the report was transparent and detailed, which was unprecedented.[23]

In 2010, the number of departments submitting detailed departmental budget in Shanghai reached up to 100 from 35. The budgets of all municipal departments except classified and state secret ones such as national defense and national security were submitted to the People's Congress for examination. The municipal People's Congress announced that it would work with relevant departments and some deputies to track the whole process of 2009 departmental budget of the municipal educational commission, understanding in real time compilation, implementation, and final accounts of the departmental budget. In the term of the current standing committee, the municipal People's Congress will annually choose one or two key departments to track and supervise the whole process of departmental budget.

Section 3. Avoid Blank Spot of Supervision in the Process of Budgetary Implementation

1. Carry Out Real Audit and Supervision

In many areas, the local People's Congress is making more and more progress in guiding and leading the audit departments to participate in budgetary supervision. In some areas meeting of directors of the standing committee of the People's Congress instructs the audit departments to carry out special investigations into the use of the funds for designated departments and special projects and report the audit results; the deputies and members of the standing committee of the People's Congress query and inquire questions found in the audit in accordance with legal

[23] Zhao Li-wei, Shao Jian-bin. Studies on the Ways to Strengthen Budget Supervision with the Example of Guangdong Phenomenon. *People's Congress Research*, 2004, (6): 38.

procedures and arranges special investigations and holds hearings for major problems or specific issues.

Especially, some local People's Congress or their deputies begin to consider and discuss the institutional issues on national audit system when they put forward the requirements for the audit departments. For instance, on the 19th meeting of the 11th standing committee of the People's Congress of Guangzhou City in August 2000, when reviewing the financial budget and other financial revenues and expenditures of Guangzhou City in 1999, many members were not satisfied with the audit results as they believed that the audit report did not truly reflect the audit results. The committee members pointed out that the People's Congress's supervision on the government is an important function granted by the Constitution and laws, and if it does not obtain information, how can the People's Congress exercise the power of supervision.

The audit bureau should truthfully report the audit results in the same way as it reports to the leaders of government. The members recommended that the municipal People's Congress should promulgate some regulations to ensure that the People's Congress can instruct the audit bureau to report details of any department in order to increase its initiative of supervision and intensify supervision over the illegal use of financial funds.[24] Therefore, the government and the People's Congress need audit department in the same way with slight distinction between internal and external audit as the government is mainly expecting the audit departments to provide information of internal management within the government while the People's Congress needs more information in order to supervise the government.

Moreover, the audit department can often find improper administrative acts and decisions of the leaders of government and under this situation affiliated relation of the audit department will play a different role, as the principal leaders of government will prevent the audit department from making audit reports against them (or the government leadership). The People's Congress will also expect the audit department to provide more real and detailed information reflecting implementation of the

[24]Yang Su-chang. On Development and Deepening of the Relations between the People's Congress and the National Audit Bureau. *People's Congress Research*, 2003, (10): 5–9.

financial budget regardless of the government leaders involved. China should consider two types of audit organs, as the audit department subordinate to the People's Congress is primarily responsible for external supervision over the government, while the other audit department subordinate to the government acts as a consulting department responsible for internal management.

In terms of institutional ownership audit department is an administrative agency and the People's Congress cannot directly conduct the department, generally only referring to the audit reports. However, in terms of the supervisory characteristic of the audit, it is not a reasonable institutional design to make the audit department subordinate to the government. On the contrary, it should be led by the People's Congress as an independent agency to supervise the government over public financial revenues and expenditures.

Provincial public finance can be audited either by audit bureau of the central government or by the audit department of provincial government. The results of the audit and investigation into financial budget management in 18 provinces and autonomous regions made by the national audit bureau in 2009 show that in 10 provinces and cities, over 60 billion Yuan of granting fees for the land-use right are not included in the budget. The director of financial audit office of the audit bureau says in accordance with the national regulations, from January 1, 2007, all the income of granting fees for the land-use right should be included in the budget for management in full. Audit by test-checking in ten provinces, 23 cities and 41 counties in 2007 show that 84.826 billion Yuan of non-tax revenues are not included in the general budget and fund budget for management, which consist of 62.642 billion Yuan income of granting fees for the land-use right and 4.456 billion Yuan income of state-owned capital operation.

National audit bureau in 2009 investigated financial management of 2008 fiscal year and the first half of 2009 in 15 provinces of Beijing, Hebei, Shanxi, Heilongjiang, Shanghai, Jiangsu, Jiangxi, Shandong, Guangdong, Chongqing, Sichuan, Yunnan, Gansu, Qinghai, Ningxia and two independent cities of Dalian and Shenzhen. In 17 provinces and autonomous regions, 62.538 billion Yuan of non-tax revenues that have been collected were not timely paid into the treasury for budgetary management as required and were even kept in interim accounts or non-budgetary accounts of the departments of tax collection. In 17 provinces and autonomous regions, except treasury deposit accounts of the financial departments, 1197 accounts were opened in commercial banks, in which 920 should be cleaned up, more than 50 per province in average.

Many local governments are involved in improper land grant without payment. In 12 provinces and 26 autonomous cities and counties up to 75 billion Yuan of granting fees for the land-use right were not collected. 1270 departments out of 8561 in Shaanxi Province, in 2007, were audited. According to the audit report, 14.838 billion Yuan was improper and the audit helped save 15.24 billion of costs in which 424 million Yuan was turned over to the government and 1.096 billion Yuan was returned to the original channels and the audit avoided loss of 54.35 million Yuan and adopted 3666 recommendations.[25]

In 2007 Zhejiang provincial audit office found 17.3 billion of improper funds. By checking budgetary implementation in 15 provincial departments and 69 subordinate departments 641 million Yuan of funds were found improper. Social security funds of enterprise employees' basic pension insurance, basic medical insurance for urban workers, unemployment insurance, industrial injury insurance, and maternity insurance were simultaneously audited and 787 million Yuan of improper funds were found.[26] Regarding these improper funds, in the current context of the administrative management system in China, implementation of the financial budget is an extremely complex process, in which only the professional departments such as audit department can formally and accurately audit the implementation of the budget and then put forward opinions and suggestions for supervision. So, if the People's Congress wants to strengthen the supervision of financial budget, it must properly make use of the powers of the audit department.

2. Improve Real-Time Supervision

Since the process of budgetary implementation is dynamic, supervision of the People's Congress should also be dynamic in order to keep abreast of

[25] Ming Li, Tao Yan. Shaanxi Audit Departments Found 14.8 Billion Yuan of Irregular Funds. *Xi'an Evening News*, 2007, 9 (26).

[26] Li Guan-nan. Zhejiang Audit Departments Found 17.3 Billion Yuan of Illegal Funds in 2006. *Zhejiang Online*, 2007, 9 (26).

information of the budgetary implementation. Real-time dynamic supervision consists of internal and external channels. The range of social supervision of the government budget is very wide as the media, network, social organizations, and individuals all have the right to supervise. It can be done in many ways as exposure, criticism, suggestions, and evaluation can all play a role in disclosure, inspection, and supervision. The People's Congress and its standing committee should be good at guiding social supervision in playing the role of social supervision. To create a supervision platform, it needs to improve the channels of collecting opinions of supervision in many ways such as on the internet, newspaper or magazine, setting up columns and evaluation forms for assessing the services, and efficiency of the government departments.[27]

In September 2004, Guangdong Province launched a real-time online financial supervision system, which facilitates the department of finance and economy committee of the Guangdong provincial People's Congress to directly connect to the centralized treasury payment system for real-time online supervision over implementation of provincial budgets. Through the real-time online financial supervision system, the department of finance and economy committee of the People's Congress and the deputies could retrieve information of every sum of centralized treasury payment in a certain departmental budget in time, thus enhancing supervision of the People's Congress over implementation of departmental budgets.

With the development of the socialist market economic system, the government's fiscal behavior is becoming more frequent and complex and it is difficult for the People's Congress to truly and effectively supervise the financial expenses just by examining the reports with thousands of words and on the two annual meeting or by routine audit of several large projects. In the future, each penny of financial expenditures should be immediately supervised by the People's Congress. Staff of the budgetary supervision office of the financial and economic committee of the provincial People's Congress can clearly realize the potential of financial funds of the departments by simply clicking a mouse, including government

[27] Zhao Wen. *Concise Reading of Budget Examination and Supervision of Local People's Congress*, Shanghai: Fudan University Press, 2008: 223.

procurement, payment of wages and procurement of official cars. Guangdong centralized treasury payment system is like an account book of the government, which keeps records of tens of billions of Yuan of financial expenditure of the government.

The financial and economic committee of the People's Congress can directly search and supervise the financial expenditure of the government on the internet through the system. By means of modern technologies this new initiative truly turns the government finances into transparent counter. Its creative significance is that the People's Congress' supervision of financial expenditures is changing from supervision of periodic statements to real-time supervision, from supervision of the results to comprehensive supervision of all the aspects, and from extensive supervision and detailed supervision.[28] It connected the standing committee of the People's Congress, the financial department and the treasury with a network and created a platform where the People's Congress and the government can share information so that the government's every movement is completely under the supervision of the People's Congress and understood by the public. The network of the People's Congress and the financial departments enables the People's Congress grasp in time the spending of financial funds, strengthen its dynamic supervision over budgetary implementation, and enhance transparency of implementation and effectiveness of supervision.[29]

---

[28] Supervising Government Expenditure through Glass Counter and the People's Congress Supervision Defending Public Finance http://www.southcn.com/news/gdnews/sz/rd50/gdxx/200503150238.htm (Accessed on March 15, 2005).

[29] Yang Xiu-zhi. *People's Congress Supervision over Budget Implementation and Improvement in Legislation*, Beijing: China University of Political Science, 2009: 33.

Conclusion

Power to tax involves the power to destroy.

— John Marshall

Modern constitutional system focuses on establishment of the balance of powers and limited government. The budget is related to critical interests concerning citizens, representative agencies, and the government in modern state governance. Public budget essentially is not only a technical issue but also a political issue involving the game between the public powers of the government and civil rights of the people. Budgetary supervision is a country's political proposition and of course a constitutional issue at the normative level. Regulations on supervision power of public budget have become an indicator to evaluate constitutional governance of a nation.

For a long time, the nature of public finance is not deeply rooted and there is no regulatory practice of the people's participation in decision-making and management of public financial revenues and expenditures. Although four versions of the Constitution have mentioned the concept of the budget and to some extent developed a simple budgetary supervision system, the budget has always been a concept in the planned economy and fails to define legal relationship with the People's Congress and the public, not to mention protecting citizens' right to know financial and budget information and powers of participation in budget decision-making and budgetary supervision in view of the constitutional aspect.

The Organic Law of the Local People's Congress and the Local People's Governments passed in 1979, the Budget Law passed in 1994, and the Law of the Supervision of Standing Committee of People's Congress at Various Levels passed in 2006 are the highest regulatory laws for powers of budgetary supervision of the People's Congress and provide specific contents and procedures of budgetary supervision. From the end of the last century to the beginning of this century the provincial People's Congress in various provinces also have made local laws and regulations such as regulations on budgetary supervision and rules for government information openness; especially, the provinces have also promulgated local regulations to implement the Supervision Law to provide the specific content of budgetary supervision based on the regional characteristics.

These laws and regulations have laid a legal basis for improving the budgetary supervision system of the provincial People's Congress and protecting citizens' right of budgetary supervision to know budget information and to participate in budgetary decision-making. Powers of budgetary supervision and making budgetary decision of the provincial People's Congress gradually established and in some provinces powers of budgetary amendment of the provincial People's Congress are realized so that it systematically ensures the symbolic significance of the powers of budgetary supervision. However, even if the People's Congress is an organ of power, it fails to build essential power of supervision over the government public budget as the laws do not provide clear regulations and operational procedures, leading the power of budgetary supervision of the People's Congress to be invalid. Actually the concept of budget came true only after the reform and opening up in the late 1980s when the system of financial responsibility was introduced. The power of budgetary supervision of the People's Congress was not accurately defined in the Constitution until 1982. What is more, the citizens' power of budgetary supervision has not been accurately defined yet.

This book absorbs various results of many scholars of law, politics, and economics, both at home and abroad to explore the problems of the budgetary supervision system of the provincial People's Congress and analyzes the causes. First, problems existing in the supervision process can be summarized as follows: Constitutional awareness is weak in institutional construction, and improvement of the legal system and information exchange system are not smooth. Second, information disclosure is the basis of budgetary supervision, yet there is no information openness system which matches the budgetary supervision system in China. Incomplete information openness and difficulties in accessing the budget information for the People's Congress and the public has become a major obstacle in improving the budgetary supervision system of the provincial People's Congress. The most fundamental problem of budgetary supervision of the provincial People's Congress in China is that the supervision is not substantive. With normative analysis methods and empirical case studies, the author analyzes the causes of insubstantial budgetary supervision from configuration of the powers, legal bases for operation, and limitations of the real political system.

The budgetary process is a political process in which a variety of agencies and citizens participate and thus difficulties of budgetary supervision lie in changes and improvement of the political powers, that is to say the balance between the various powers and rights. First, this book is designed to respond to a difficult problem — how the laws can protect the position of the People's Congress's in budgetary supervision in political operation, which is the basis of changing the *status quo* of insubstantial budgetary supervision of the People's Congress. On the one hand, it needs to regulate the exercise of powers of the government and the provincial Party committee in budgetary process in terms of the budgetary supervision system and on the other hand it needs to promote the position of the People's Congress in the whole process of budgetary supervision, especially the statutory powers of intervention in budgetary decision-making, powers of amendments in budgetary compilation, and powers of investigation in budgetary implementation. If the People's Congress can be effectively involved in supervision in the key stages of the budgetary process, the power of budgetary supervision of the People's Congress granted by the Supervision Law can be achieved.

Given that the most serious problem of budgetary supervision of the provincial People's Congress in China is insubstantial supervision, it needs to explore rational allocation of the power of budgetary supervision granted by the Constitution from the legal perspective, namely, balance between the powers of the People's Congress and various participation of other powers in the budgetary process, otherwise it would be unable to change the current situation. In different budgetary processes, the powers involved in the budget are different and above all the People's Congress shall solve issues of power allocation in the provincial budgetary process where the powers impose impacts on the budgetary decision-making and should take part in the process of making decisions from the very beginning as early as possible so that the supervision can play an essential role in the whole budgetary process.

The first issue to be addressed is regulation on exercise of powers of the Party committee and the government in the budgetary decision-making process and a legal system to ensure their compulsory cooperation with the People's Congress. Since a variety of powers are involved in the game at the most critical stage of making budgetary decision, it needs to define mutual relations of the various powers and their respective boundaries in the budgetary decision-making process, that is to say, any power shall not make fundamental decisions for the budget without balance and check of other powers.

In the process of making budgets, lack of draft budget amendment power is one of the major deficiencies of the current legal provisions. As the public have much more louder voice to demand the local People's Congress to strengthen supervision over the government budget, although some provinces have made regulations on budgetary amendments in the local laws and regulations on budgetary supervision, there is no systematically normative or comprehensive provision. As the draft budget amendment is not a simple mechanism of voting, it requires a set of reasonable systems to specify the political consultation mechanism in the draft budget and only in this way can the public opinion be truly reflected in the process of making the budget, and the nature of publicity of the budget can really be demonstrated. Of course, as it seems that the main body of exercise of the power of budgetary supervision to a certain degree can also make mistakes of opportunism, the Constitution should consider granting the power of budgetary supervision to the People's Congress while at the same time designing a system to prevent improper acts of the people's representatives.

Second, as budget information disclosure plays a fundamental role in the entire budgetary supervision system, it needs to provide legal protection for improving the system of budget information openness. When the budgetary system reform, budget information disclosure, and budgetary supervision system cannot well-coordinate in their own process of improvement, it will be necessary to explore a system platform for information disclosure of the provincial budget and really have governments' capacities of public governance recognized and supervised by the public. The laws on budget information disclosure are very limited and the requirements of integrity and validity of budget information disclosure are not sound or operational in practice.

The major difficulty in solving the issue of lack of budgetary transparency is to urge the government to fulfill duties at the legal level in order to truly transform self-controlled government to limited government. The current Constitution only stresses citizens' obligations of paying taxes but does not define obligations of budget information openness for the government. To really solve the problem at the legal level, the first thing is to make exploration in providing constitutional protection for the citizens' right to know budget information and legal relationships in budget information openness. Basic laws shall also specify the principles, scope, procedures, responsibilities, and relief measures of budget information openness to protect the people's right to know and consolidate the foundation for democratic politics of national development.

It needs to pay attention to integrity, standardization, and timeliness of disclosure during the process of specific information disclosure. Legal protection is always the most solid foundation for budgetary supervision. As the local regulations on provincial budgetary supervision are mostly made prior to the national Supervision Law and they need to be modified according to the requirements of new social situations, various provinces also need to develop new unified local laws and regulations on budgetary supervision in accordance with the national budgetary laws, regulations, and rules with unified standards and specifications for budget information openness.

Third, as budgetary supervision is involved in the whole budgetary process, one of the most important reasons of insubstantial budgetary supervision is lack of substantive regulations on supervisory procedures in practice. To solve the issue that power of budgetary supervision of the People's Congress is weak, it needs to improve the supervisory procedures in the whole process of budgetary decision-making, compilation, and implementation. In terms of the system, the most urgent thing to be improved is to strengthen legislation of the budgetary process by for the People's Congress as both in the stage of making decision and amending the draft budget it needs strict legislation to protect the power of intervention in supervision of the People's Congress.

Transition from high centralization to fragmented decentralization of Chinese provincial budgetary decision-making system causes great trouble to budgetary supervision of the People's Congress. As a result, a concentrated budgetary agency was never built and expenditure decentralization has been too serious. In this context, to strengthen the participation of the People's Congress in the budgetary decision-making is critical to achievement of eventual effectiveness of budgetary supervision. At the same time, it comes down to another important aspect, namely, to strengthen reunification of the budgetary powers. Strengthening the financial unification and budgetary supervision simultaneously will help establish the foundation of the effective supervision over the government budgetary acts of the People's Congress and improve the system to ensure that the People's Congress can participate in the budgetary process at the very beginning, collect the budgetary compilation information, make proposals for adjustment and make consultation for the government.

The People's Congress is the statutory body of budgetary supervision and its inner structural configuration and qualities of the deputies to the People's Congress are the external basis of operation of the budgetary supervision system. First of all, the professional qualities of the deputies and the organization of the People's Congress need transformation to meet the requirements of fulfilling the important mission of budgetary supervision as a representative agency. This issue is not studied and analyzed in detail in this book and the author expects to make extensive empirical studies in the future based on more empirical data, such as specific proportions of the deputies to the People's Congress, including the proportion of officials, Party members and scholars, professional and full-time deputies, assistant institutions and staff. Second, the topics such as cooperation and support of the People's Congress with the government in reform of the budgetary system, making use of the social forces in playing the role of checks and balances based on openness and explorations in construction of the system through which the citizens participate in budgetary supervision deserve further researches.

With further normalization of the central government management, local governance will be critical to political development in the future and improvement of the budgetary supervision system of the provincial People's Congress will promote legal construction of the local government, which will necessarily touch on the game of standardization of powers of the government, and the civil rights. Protection of the fundamental rights of citizens and promotion of construction of limited and responsible government of rule of law will further improve the political system in which the people are the masters, thus truly building a socialist country under the rule of law.

Bibliography

45 Departments in Beijing Will Disclose their Budgets Online this Month. *Beijing News*, 2010, 5 (21).

Aaron Wildavsky. *The New Politics of the Budgetary Process*, Shanghai: Shanghai University of Finance and Economics Press, 2006.

Aaron Wildavsky. *Budget: Comparing Theory*, Shanghai: Shanghai University of Finance and Economics Press, 2009.

Aaron Wildavsky, Naomi Caiden. *The New Politics of the Budgetary Process*, Beijing: Peking University Press, 2009.

All Provincial Departmental Budgets Disclosed to the People's Congress in Hunan. *People's Daily*, 2009, 1 (19).

All the Shanghai Municipal Department Budgets will be Submitted to the People's Congress for Examination. *First Financial News*, 2011, 1 (5).

Bai Yan-feng. *On Configuration of Tax Rights — Vertical Division of Chinese Tax Rights*, Beijing: China Financial and Economic Publishing House, 2006.

Beijing Municipal Government Departmental Budgets will be Fully Disclosed Next Year. *Beijing News*, 2010, 5 (11).

Buck, A.E. The Development of the Budget Idea in the United States. *Annal of the American Academy of Political and Social Science, Vol. 113, Competency and Economy in Public Expenditure* (May, 1924).

Budgetary Supervision is still Blank, Why there is Little Improvement in Provincial Financial Transparency? *China Youth Daily*, 2010, 7 (22).

Cai Ding-jian. Constitutional Development in Social Transition of China. *Journal of the East China University of Politics and Law*, 2006, (4).

Cai Ding-jian. *The People's Congress System in China* (Fourth Edition), Beijing: Law Press, 2003.

Cai Ding-jian. Approaches and Technologies of the Reform of Public Budget. *Chinese Reform*, 2007, (6).

Carol Pateman. *Participation and Democratic Theory*, Shanghai: Shanghai Century Publishing Group, 2006.

Chen Shi-yi, Zhang Jun. Did Financial Decentralization Improve Efficiency of the Expenditures of Chinese Local Government? Evidence from Provincial Governments from 1978 to 2004. *Competition for Growth — Politics and Economics of the Growth in China*, Shanghai: Shanghai People's Publishing House, 2008.

China Development Research Foundation. Public Budgets Reading, Beijing: China Development Press, 2008.

Dai Ji-tao. Legal Construction of Civil Participation in Budget: from Specification to System. *Journal of Guangdong Institute of Public Administration*, 2010, (6).

Deng Yu-Wen. Audit Storm Urging Budget Reform. *International Finance*, 2005, 7 (4): 5.

Ellen Rubin. *Public Budget Politics: Revenues and Expenditure, Debts and Balance*, Beijing: China Renmin University Press, 2001.

Financial and Economic Committee of Beijing People's Congress Review the Report of the Government on Performance of the Spending for the First Time. *Beijing News*, 2010, 1 (21).

Gay B. Peters. *Politics of Taxation*, Nanjing: Jiangsu People's Publishing House, 2008.

Ge Ke-chang. *Fundamental Issues of Tax (Collection of Financial and Constitutional Articles)*, Beijing: Peking University Press, 2004.

Glass Counter Closely Supervise Spendings of the Government, the People's Congress Supervision Defends Public Finances. *Southern Website*, 2009, 10 (25).

Guo Jian-fei. *Performance Budget — New Perspective of Governance Mode in Pudong*, Beijing: China Finance and Economics Publishing House, 2008.

Han Da-yuan. *The Constitution*, Beijing: Higher Education Press, 2006.

He Bang-jing. *China's Financial Supervision System*, Beijing: Economic Science Press, 2008.

He Jun-zhi. Theoretical Origins and International Practice of Budget Transparency. *Journal of China National School of Administration*, 2008.

Hebei will Actively Promote Fiscal Budget Disclosure This Year. *Shijiazhuang City Network*, 2010, 4 (20).

Hua Guo-qing. On the Taxpayers' Right to Know and its Legal Protection. *Jurists*, 2006, (2).

Huang Pei-hua. *China: National Development and Local Finance*, Beijing: CITIC Publishing House, 2003.

Huang Yan. *On Development of Local Public Finance*, Beijing: China Social Sciences Press, 2007.

Huang Zhen-ping. *How Deputies Exercise Budget Examination and Supervision*, Beijing: China Financial and Economic Publishing House, 2009.

James M. Buchanan. *Theory of Democratic Finance*, Beijing: Commercial Press, 2002.

Janet M. Kelly, William C. Raven Barker. *Local Government Performance Budget*, Shanghai: Shanghai University of Finance and Economics Press, 2007.

Jia Kang. *On Local Financial Problems*, Beijing: Economic Science Press, 2004.

Jian Hong. *On Public Financial Decision-making and Supervision System*, Beijing: China Financial and Economic Publishing House, 2008.

Jiang Hong. *Report on China's Financial Transparency — Assessment of Provincial Financial Information Disclosure (2009)*, Shanghai: Shanghai University of Finance and Economics Press, 2009a.

Jiang Hong. Studies of Budget Transparency. Studies on Several Major Issues about Draft Amendments to China's Budget Law, Symposium of the Major Issues about Amendment to Budget Law, 2009b.

Jiang Long. Theoretical Origins of Financial Supervision in Public Finance. *Financial Research*, 2001.

Jiao Jian-guo. Budget Mechanism Theory: Analysis from the Economic, Political, Legal, Financial and Decision-making Perspectives. *Journal of China National School of Administration*, 2002, (4): 79.

John Mick Purcell. *Public Financial Management: Analysis and Application*, Beijing: China Renmin University Press, 2005.

Jonathan Kahn. *Budgeting Democracy — National Building and Citizenship in America (1890–1928)*, Shanghai: Shanghai People's Publishing House, 2008, (8): 180.

Li Bu-yun. *Comparative Studies of the Constitution*, Beijing: Law Press, 1998.

Li Chuan-xi. Assessment of Theory of Public Choice and the Doctrine of Separation of Constitutional Powers and Evaluation on the Improvement of Budgetary supervision System in China. *Theory and Reform*, 2003.

Li Fan. *Wenling Test and Public Budget Reform of the Local Government in China*, Beijing: Intellectual Property Press, 2009.

Li Guan-nan. Zhejiang Audit Departments Found 17.3 Billion Yuan of Illegal Funds in 2006. *Zhejiang Online*, 2007, 9 (26).

Li Jin-hua. Audit Report on Implementation of the Central Budget and Other Financial Revenues and Expenditures in 2003. Communique of the Tenth Meeting of the Tenth Standing Committee of the National People's Congress, 2004.

Li Wei-guang. Budget Transparency: Choice at a New Crossroad. *People Website — People's Forum*, 2010a, 3 (16).

Li Wei-guang. Chinese Tax: Blood of Morality Should Flow. *South Wind*, 2010b.

Li Yan. Disclosure and Transparency of Financial Information is the Basis for Budgetary supervision and Management. *Financial Research*, 2010, (6).

Li Yan. Exploration in Analysis of Budget Transparency from the Perspective of Democratic Supervision. *Journal of Central University of Finance and Economics*, 2007, (12).

Lin Mu-hua. Reshape Budgetary Powers of the People's Congress — Based on Surveys in a Province. *Public Administration Review*, 2008, (4).

Lin Shang-li. Financial Basis of Democratic Centralism — An Analysis of Chinese National Construction. *Social Sciences*, 2006, (11).

Lin Yi-fu, Liu Zhi-qiang. China's Financial Decentralization and Economic Growth. *Journal of Peking University (Philosophy and Social Science)*, 2000.

Liu Hui. *Budgetary Supervision and Democratic Growth: Analysis of the National People's Congress Budgetary Supervision System from the Political Perspective (1978–2006)*, Shanghai: Fudan University, 2008: 98.

Liu Jian-wen. *The Finance under Rule of Law from the Democratic Perspective*, Beijing: Peking University Press, 2006.

Liu Jian-wen. Constitutionalism and Chinese Financial Democracy. *Tax Research*, 2008, (4).

Liu Jian-wen, Xiong Wei. On Development and Improvement of China's Budget Law. *Administrative Law Review*, 2001a, (4).

Liu Jian-wen, Xiong Wei. Reform of Budget Examination and Approval System and Improvement of China's Budget Law. *Jurist*, 2001b, (6).

Liu Li. *Constitutional Control of the Tax Powers*, Beijing: Law Press, 2006.

Liu Rong. *On Tax Reform from the Constitutional Perspective*, Beijing: Law Press, 2008.

Liu Shou-gang. *Financial Logic of National Growth — Financial Transformation and Political Development in Modern China*, Tianjin: Tianjin People's Publishing House, 2009.

Liu Wei. On the Path of Improving the Budgetary Supervision System of the People's Congress. *The People's Congress Research*, 2008, (1): 17.

Liu Xiao-Bing, Deng Shu-lian, Wen Jiao-xiu. The Evaluation of China's Provincial Fiscal Transparency in 2010 (2010). *Journal of Shanghai University of Finance and Economics*, 2010, (6): 56.

Liu Xiao-bing. Improve the Status of the Audit Department, Implement the National People's Congress Budgetary Supervision. *Journal of Shanghai University of Finance and Economics*, 2008, (3).

Local Debts at Risk — To Get Rid of Institutional Obstacles in Local Government Economic Development is the Basic Solution. *China Business Times*, 2010.

Locke. *Theory of Government* (*Part II*), Beijing: Commercial Press, 1964.

Ma Guo-xian. *On Theory of Government Budget and Policies of Performance*, Beijing: China Financial and Economic Publishing House, 2008.

Ma Hai-tao. *Government Budget Management*, Shanghai: Fudan University Press, 2003.

Ma Jun. *Chinese Public Budget Reform: Rationalization and Democratization*, Central Compilation and Translation Press, 2005.

Ma Jun. Politics of the Budget Reform in China: Achievements and Plight. *Journal of Sun Yat-sen University* (*Philosophy and Social Science*), 2007, (3).

Ma Jun. Economic and Social Changes and Transformation of Governance: Reform of the U.S. Progressive Era. *Public Management Research*, 2008, (6).

Ma Jun, Hou Yi-lin. Informal System of Provincial Budgets in China: A Theory Framework of Transaction Cost. *Economic Research*, 2004, (10).

Ma Jun, Lin Mu-hua. Powers of Budget Amendment of the Modern Parliament. *Calls for the Public Budget*, Beijing: Central Compilation and Translation Press, 2008.

Ma Jun, Luo Wan-ping. Civil Participation in Budget: Experiences for U.S. Local Government. *Journal of Central China Normal University* (*Humanities and Social Sciences*), 2006, (7).

Ma Jun, Niu Mei-li. Reconstruction of Chinese Public Budgetary System: The Power and the Relationship-Based on Researches of Local Budgets. *Observation of China's Development*, 2007, (2).

Ma Jun, Zhao Zao-zao. Options of the Goals of Budget Reform in China. *Journal of China Central Normal University* (*Social Science Edition*), 2005, (5).

Ma Jun, Zhou Yan. On Decision-making System of Chinese Provincial Government Investment — A Case Study. *Public Management Research*, 2008, (4).

Ma, Hou Yi-lin. Policy Process and Budget Process of Provincial Budget in China: Surveys in two Provinces. *Economic and Social Systems Research*, 2005, (5).

Mao Shou-long, Li Mei. *Economic Analysis of Limited Government*, Shanghai: Shanghai Joint Publishing, 2000.

Mill, J. S. *Considerations on Representative Government*, Beijing: Commercial Press, 2007.

Ming Li, Tao Yan. Shaanxi Audit Departments Found 14.8 Billion Yuan of Irregular Funds. *Xi'an Evening News*, 2007, 9 (26).

Ministry of Finance Plans to Promote Unified Disclosure of Local Budget. *Jinan Daily*, 2010, 1 (22).

National Development and Research Institute of Peking University, Issues in China, Shanghai: Shanghai People's Publishing House, 2010.

Niu Mei-li. Citizenship and Public Budget — The Road of Democratic Governance. *Public Administration Review*, 2008, (1).

Official Kindergarten is the 'Tail' of Planned Economy. *People's Daily*, 2011, 1 (26).

'Official Kindergarten Supported by Finance' will Continue to Exist or not. *China Youth Daily*, 2011, 2 (2).

Qian Jun-wen. *Constitutional Control of State Taxing Powers*, Beijing: Law Press, 2007.

Qiu Zhu-xiang. *Tax-sharing and Constitutionalism — Value and Logic of Decentralization of Central and Local Financial Powers*, Beijing: Intellectual Property Press, 2008.

Quan Cheng-xiang. Constitutional Configuration of the State Financial Powers. *Hunan Forum*, 2008, (1).

Ren Xi-rong. Budgetary Supervision and Financial Democracy: Growth of the Power of Budgetary Supervision of the People's Congress. *Journal of University of Political Science of East China*, 2009.

Ren Xi-rong. Systematic Analysis of Growth of the Power of Budgetary Supervision of the Local People's Congress — An Example of Constitutional Development in China. *Journal of Social Science of Jilin University*, 2010, (7).

Report on China's Fiscal Transparency — The Evaluation of Provincial Fiscal Information Disclosure, Shanghai: Shanghai University of Finance and Economics Press, 2009.

Rigid Budget Constraints, the First Step of Restricting the Powers of the Government. *South Wind*, 2010, (2).

Shen Zong-ling. *Modern Western Constitution*, Beijing: Peking University Press, 1992.

Steven J. Diener. *Unusual Times: Americans in the Progressive Era*, Shanghai: Shanghai People's Publishing House, 2008.

Sun Kai. On Public Budgetary Supervision Mechanism. *Financial Research*, 2007, (10).

Sun Zhe. *On National People's Congress System*, Beijing: Law Press, 2004.

The Results of the Audits and Investigations into Financial Budget Management in 17 Provinces and Autonomous Regions. The National Audit Bureau, 2010.

Tian Bi-yao. China Budget Disclosure Road Map. *People's Congress Research*, 2010.

Tian Yi, Duan Wen. New Situiation of the People's Congress: Party Secretary is the Director of the People's Congress. *21st Century Economic Report*, 2003, 3 (7).

Tong Zhi-Wei. *The Constitution*, Beijing: Tsinghua University Press, 2008.

U.S. Government Performance Evaluation System, Beijing: Economic Management Press, 2004.

Vincent Ostrom, Robert Bishi. *U.S. Local Government*, Beijing: Peking University Press, 2004.

Wan Feng, Xie Lin-mei, He Bao-qing. Jiangxi Province Issued the Opinions to Further Promote Administrative Affairs Openness of the Financial Departments. *Jiangxi Daily*, 2006, 4 (15).

Wang Jin-feng. Regulations of Financial Powers from the Constitutional View. *Local Finance Studies*, 2009, (6).

Wang Shaoguang, Ma Jun. To 'National Budget' — Financial Transformation and Nation-building. *Public Administration Review*, 2008, (1).

Wang Shao-guang. *Enlightenment of the U.S. Progressive Era*, Beijing: China Financial and Economic Publishing House, 2002, (6).

Wang Shao-guang. From Tax Country to Budget Country. *Reading*, 2007, (10).

Wang Sheng. *Financial Supervision Theory — On Exploration and System Design*, Beijing: Economic Management Press, 2009.

Wang Shi-tao. Constitutional Interpretation of Chinese Finance. *Journal of Gansu Political Science and Law Institute*, 2008, (2).

Wang Shi-tao. Revision of the Budget Law and Improvement of the Legal System of Budgetary supervision. *Financial Studies*, 2005, (3).

Wang Shu-Jie. *On Legislative Supervision Model of Government Budget*, Beijing: China Financial and Economic Publishing House, 2008.

Wang Yong-li, Wang Sheng-fang. Boundaries of Examination of Budget Amendments of the Legislature. *Journal of Fujian Institute of Political Science & Law*, 2003, (10).

Wei Jian-guo. *Formation of Constitutional System and Rise of Modern Britain*, Beijing: Law Press, 2006.

Wen Bing-xun. Administrative Control, Political Control and Public Budget — on the Public Budget Reform in China. *Journal of Social Science of Hunan Normal University*, 2007, (3).

Why Official Kindergarten Cannot be Abolished? *Beijing News*, 2011, 1 (29).

Willoughby, W.F. The Budget as an Instrument of Political Reform. *Proceedings of the Academy of the Political Science in the City of New York*, Vol. 8, National Conference on War Economy (July 1918).

Wilson. *Congressional Government: A Study in American Politics*, Beijing: Commercial Press, 1986.

Xu Chong-de. *The Constitution* (Fourth Edition), Beijing: China People's University Press, 2009.

Xu Hong. *Financial Control and Financial Democracy*, Shanghai: Fudan University, 2006.

Xu Meng-zhou, Ye Shan. On System Arrangements of the Financial Transfer Payment Between Governments. *Social Sciences*, 2010, (7).

Xu Shu-na. Analysis of the Environments of the Local People's Congress Budgetary Supervision System. *Journal of Shanghai University of Finance and Economics*, 2008, (6).

Xu Shu-na. On Budgetary Supervision of the People's Congress. Studies on Several Major Issues about Draft Amendments to China's Budget Law, 2009.

Xu Yang-guang. *Legal Analysis of the Financial Transfer Payment System*, Beijing: Peking University Press, 2009.

Yan Hai. Budget Democracy: Construction Based on the Power of Budget Approval. *Chongqing Social Science*, 2007, (4).

Yan Hai. Multiple Supervision over the Implementation of the Budget in Japan Based on Constitutional System. *Jiangsu Social Sciences*, 2010, (2).

Yang Hai-Kun. *Basic Constitutional Theory*, Beijing: China Democratic and Legal System Press, 2007.

Yang Jun-chang. *Public Budget: Key to Government Reform*, Beijing: China Financial and Economic Publishing House, 2008.

Yang Su-chang. On Development and Deepening of the Relations between the People's Congress and the National Audit Bureau. *People's Congress Research*, 2003, (10).

Yang Xiu-zhi. *People's Congress Supervision over Budgetary Implementation and Improvement in Legislation*, Beijing: China University of Political Science, 2009.

Yang Zhi-yong, Yang Zhi-gang. *30 Years of Reform of Financial System in China*, Shanghai: Shanghai People's Publishing House, 2008.

Ye Qian, Wang Pan. Deputies of the Local People's Congress Actively Promote to Disclose Provincial Budget to the Whole Society. *Xinhua News Agency*, 2010.

Yu Li-yan. All the 100 Municipal Departments in Shanghai will Deliver Their Budgets to the People's Congress for Examination Next Year. *Oriental Morning Post*, 2009, 5 (14).

Zeng Jun-ping, Shang Hai-quan. Studies on the Issue of Budget Amendment. Studies on Several Major Issues about Draft Amendments to China's Budget Law, 2009.

Zeng Jun-ping. The Budget Amendment Rights Need Strict Rules and Norms. *Journal of Shanghai University of Finance and Economics*, 2008, 3.

Zeng Jun-ping. The People's Congress Budgetary Decision-making, Opportunistic Behaviors and Constitutional Constraints. *Journal of Shanghai University of Finance and Economics*, 2009, (2).

Zhang Jin-song. *On Supervisory of the People's Congress from the Constitutional Perspective*, Guangzhou: Guangdong People's Publishing House, 2009.

Zhang Jun. *The Reform Unknown to the Public*, Beijing: CITIC Publishing House, 2010.

Zhang Qian-fan. *Constitutionalism, Rule of Law and Economic Development*, Beijing: Peking University Press, 2004.

Zhang Qian-fan. *Introduction to the Constitution — Principles and Applications* (Second Edition), Beijing: Law Press, 2008.

Zhang Shou-wen. *On Tax Law*, Beijing: Peking University Press, 2005.

Zhang Wen-li. *Contemporary Chinese Local Government*, Tianjin: Nankai University Press, 2009.

Zhang Wen-xian. *Jurisprudence* (Third Edition), Beijing: Law Press, 2007.

Zhang Xiao-yan. Five Major Issues of Restraint and Supervision of the Powers in China. *Chinese Party and Government Cadres Forum*, 2004, (1).

Zhao Li-wei, Shao Jian-bin. Studies on the Ways to Strengthen Budgetary supervision with the Example of Guangdong Phenomenon. *People's Congress Research*, 2004, (6).

Zhao Wen. *Concise Reading of Budget Examination and Supervision of Local People's Congress*, Shanghai: Fudan University Press, 2008.

Zhejiang. Create Precedent in the State: Announcing that the Governments' Debt Ratio in the Province Exceeded the Warning Level of 10.15%. *21st Century Business Herald*, 2010, 9 (29).

Zhejiang. Province for the First Time Disclosed Local Governments' Debts. *Southern Weekend*, 2010, 9 (30).

Zheng Yong-nian. Uneasy Anarchy in Chinese Social Grassroots, *Lianhe Zaobao*, 2009.

Zhou Gang-zhi. *On Public Finance and Constitutional State — As a Theoretical Preamble of Financial Constitution*, Beijing: Peking University Press, 2005.

Zhou Li-an. *Local Government in Transformation — Incentives and Governance of the Officials*, Shanghai: Shanghai People's Publishing House, 2008.

Zhou Shi-ya. *Researches on Financial Hierarch — Theory of Interactions of the Reform of China's Financial Hierarchy System*, Beijing: Economic Science Press, 2007.

Zhou Ye-zhong. *The Constitution* (Second Edition), Beijing: Higher Education Press, 2008.

Zhu Da-Qi. On the Purpose and Principles of Revision of the Budget Law from the Nature of State Budget in China. *China Law*, 2005, (1).

Zhu Hong-qiong. *Relationship of the Central and Local Finance and the History of its Changes*, Beijing: Economic Science Press, 2008.

Zhu Jin. Local People's Congress Budgetary Supervision: Status, Problems and Solutions. *Yangtze River Forum*, 2008, (6).

Zhu Kong-wu. *On Financial Constitutionalism*, Beijing: Law Press, 2006.

Zou Ping-xue. The Issue of Full-time Deputies to the People's Congress. *Fudan Political Science Review Vol. 6: China's Democratic Structure*, Shanghai: Shanghai People's Publishing House, 2008.